How to
Ruin
Your Life

How to Ruin Your Life

An anthology including:

How to Ruin Your Life
How to Ruin Your Love Life
How to Ruin Your Financial Life

BEN STEIN

HAY HOUSE, INC.
Carlsbad, California
London • Sydney • Johannesburg
Vancouver • Hong Kong

Published and distributed in the United States by: Hay House, Inc., P.O. Box 5100, Carlsbad, CA 92018-5100 • *Phone:* (760) 431-7695 or (800) 654-5126 • *Fax:* (760) 431-6948 or (800) 650-5115 • www.hayhouse.com • ***Published and distributed in Australia by:*** Hay House Australia Pty. Ltd., 18/36 Ralph St., Alexandria NSW 2015 • *Phone:* 612-9669-4299 • *Fax:* 612-9669-4144 • www.hayhouse.com.au • ***Published and distributed in the United Kingdom by:*** Hay House UK, Ltd. • Unit 62, Canalot Studios • 222 Kensal Rd., London W10 5BN • *Phone:* 44-20-8962-1230 • *Fax:* 44-20-8962-1239 • www.hayhouse. co.uk • ***Published and distributed in the Republic of South Africa by:*** Hay House SA (Pty), Ltd., P.O. Box 990, Witkoppen 2068 • *Phone/Fax:* 27-11-706-6612 • orders@psdprom.co.za • ***Distributed in Canada by:*** Raincoast • 9050 Shaughnessy St., Vancouver, B.C. V6P 6E5 • *Phone:* (604) 323-7100 • *Fax:* (604) 323-2600

Editorial supervision: Jill Kramer • *Design:* Tricia Breidenthal

Library of Congress Control Number: 2005926281

ISBN 13: 978-1-4019-0616-0
ISBN 10: 1-4019-0616-8

09 08 07 06   4 3 2 1
1st printing, January 2006

Printed in the United States of America

✻ ✻ ✻

For Alex, my wifey,
who has often saved me
from ruining my life;
for our son, Tommy,
whom I love to pieces;
and for all good dogs and cats.

✻ ✻ ✻

CONTENTS

HOW TO RUIN YOUR LOVE LIFE

HOW TO RUIN YOUR FINANCIAL LIFE.................235

Introduction

It should be easy to succeed. After all, there are thousands of self-help books out there telling you how to be successful. All you have to do is buy one and read it. Maybe at the most, two. But somehow, despite the wealth of these types of books out there, tens of millions are *not* successful, *are* wallowing in misery, *are* struggling and failing, and *are* drowning without a trace.

Maybe the key that will turn this lock is to no longer try to teach people how to succeed . . . but how to fail. If we follow the footsteps of the failures, and then turn back from them and go in the opposite direction, we can go toward the bright pink light of success. That, at least, is my hope. And that's why I wrote these books on how to ruin your life in general; and how to ruin your love life and your financial life, specifically.

The idea is that if you see yourself doing these things, turn around and stop doing them right now. And maybe do the opposite. Instead of fighting, make peace. Instead of spending, save. Instead of wasting your time, study and learn.

Well, it's just a thought.

Try these books on for size. If they fit, you're in real trouble. . . .

— Ben Stein

How to
Ruin
Your Life

1

Don't Learn Any Useful Skills

Make yourself useless. Don't practice decent study habits. Don't bother to acquaint yourself with history, languages, or mathematics. Don't develop any special advanced skills in law, architecture, medicine, or electrical contracting. When others sacrifice their fun times studying and attending classes, just laugh at them and stay in bed watching old movies. (In fact, a general attitude of ridiculing any genuine effort by yourself or others is also a major way to ruin your life, but more on that later.) As others learn to produce real value for the world by healing disease, making candles, applying makeup, cutting hair, or tracking inventory, don't bother to learn anything specialized or useful at all.

Yes, it's true that there's a mountain of experience and data that tell us that education and skills are the tickets to a secure, happy life. But none of that applies to *you*. Many say that others will have bigger, better lives if they acquire a skill, trade, or advanced degree. Again, none of that means a thing to you. You'll have all of the great things in life anyway. You're special, unique in every way. Just coast by on your wit and good looks. You're a wheeler and a dealer.

What kind of education did Rhett Butler have, after all? What kind did Elvis Presley have? I didn't see Madonna in grad school or P. Diddy (or whatever name he's going by these days) either. Yet look at how far they went. You'll do at least as well with good luck and fortune that just happen to drop into your lap. Make sure that you take as examples of how to ruin your life the one in a billion who succeeds *without* skills .-.-. instead of the 99 out of 100 who succeed *with* skills.

You were born knowing all you need to know, and don't you forget it. Avoid getting any education that smacks of the ordinary and the mundane. You're not ordinary. You're special, and I'll say it until you understand it. It's vital that you know that your uniqueness will get you through every crisis. You'll get by just by being *you*. Training is for the masses, not for classy folk like yourself. You're fated to be rich and famous, and you don't have to do one more thing to get it other than what you've already done. Just sit back and be your own uniquely great and lovable self.

※ ※ ※

2

Don't Learn Any Self-Discipline

Be a slob. Hey, you're not at West Point or in boot camp! You're a chilled-out, mellowed-out dude. You deserve all of the rest you can get. You need your snooze time. You need to see that movie running on the inside of your eyelids. And don't feel guilty that you're under the covers while everyone else is out working. It's not your fault that they're nine-to-five losers. Just stay in the sack and get up whenever you feel like it. Once you do get up, stay up as long as you want. There are lots of great old films on TV. Plus, there are those fabulous reruns of *Married . . . with Children* and *The Simpsons*. Nothing you could do during the day could possibly be as fruitful as watching Bart shoot down Homer for the millionth time. I mean, that's great stuff, right? And you're a real night owl, so what's the point of hitting the sack before 3 A.M.?

And don't think about the morning, because you're not going to be up then, anyway. Morning is for farmers, and I don't think a cool dude like you is going out to be cleaning out the cow stalls. Am I right?

Eat anything you want, too. Hey, you look great no matter how much you weigh. You were just born gorgeous. If you're a few hundred pounds more than those twigs in the fashion magazines, that's their problem. They're anorexic. Anyway, you have a lot on your mind, and it feels soothing to eat. So eat whatever you want whenever you want. That's your right! This country is a miracle of agricultural production, and it would be insulting to our ranchers to snub their steak and cheese and milkshakes. Plus, when you have nothing better to do, why not mosey on over to the fridge and have a bite? I mean, who's looking? You're not in a freaking police state, are you? Just eat that leftover cake or apple pie and be done with it.

Now, this part is really important: *Don't make yourself work when you'd rather play.* In fact, don't work at all if you don't feel like it. Life is short. Why should you spend even one second of it doing a darned thing you don't want to do? Hey, maybe they didn't hear, but there's a 13th Amendment to the Constitution abolishing slavery! If you did have to work, then why did they bother to fight the Civil War? What was the point of Lincoln getting assassinated if you have to sweat and toil? Forget it. You don't have to do anything you don't want to do. You're better than that. In fact, you're better than anyone or anything else on earth. You have the right to refuse to do any work you don't feel like doing. Somehow the money will come to you simply because you want it to, whether you work or not.

Don't bother to develop any sense of discipline in anything and you'll be really happy and proud of yourself! You're a big cuddly baby, and everyone will always adore you for it, even when you're a graying, paunchy, middle-aged fella.

❀ ❀ ❀

3

Convince Yourself You're the Center of the Universe

Face it: You're the only one who matters in any given situation. The truth is—and let me be the first to tell you—God went away on vacation and left you in charge! Why bother taking into account that your wife wants you to clean out the garage? Why should you even listen when your husband tells you he'd like to have a home-cooked meal for the first time in a year? So what if your parents say you haven't done any chores around the house in a month? Who gives a darn if your roommate tells you that your socks are so dirty that the smell is keeping him up at night? *Who cares?* You're the only one who counts!

Why listen to anyone else's troubles? Your problems are the ones that make the difference. If someone else's parent is sick, hey, that's their deal. If the guy who helped you with your math exam now wants you to help him wash his truck, too darned bad for that loser. Just walk right on by, but *do* expect other people to listen to you and do what you want when you want it.

So what if, after a while, no one wants to talk to you? That's just proof of what dirtbags they are. By the way, does a living, breathing deity need to have anyone to converse with? I don't think so, do you? Where *you* want to eat, where *you* want to go on vacation, where *you* want to live—that's all that matters. The whole world has got to get it straight. You come first, and there won't be any peace anywhere until everybody sure as hell knows it.

Look at it this way. Imagine that Moses came back to earth with a special 11th Commandment, and that commandment is that you're the boss for the next hundred years. Then Moses shakes your hand and gives you his staff right on worldwide TV. That's how you have to believe your destiny was shaped. Act on it minute by minute.

◈ ◈ ◈

4

※ ※ ※ ※ ※ ※

Never Accept Any Responsibility for Anything That Goes Wrong

Play the blame game. It's always someone else's fault, or else it's just bad luck. You failed your algebra class? You obviously had a lousy teacher. The other kids passed? They were brownnosers. The cops gave you a ticket because you were driving recklessly? Hey, you had a lot on your plate that day, *and* you had a late night before. You lost your job because you didn't show up on time for a week? Wow, who can work those kind of hours anyway?

Whatever it was, you didn't mean to do it wrong; anyhow, it's a hassle to have to hear someone bitching at you. (Did the pharaohs have to listen to anyone complaining about them? Did Muhammad? Or the Buddha? Then why should you?!) Basically, you have no responsibility for doing anything right, and if it doesn't go smoothly, that's someone else's problem. Your mom didn't raise you to get yelled at. There's a simple rule in this world: If it's bad, it's someone else's tough luck and you don't want to hear about it.

The world should know this by now: It's no fun to be criticized, and that means it's no fun for *you* to be criticized. You're free, indeed required, to insult and blame others. But as the official designee of the Almighty to be His Deputy on Earth, obviously you're above it all. That's clear, right? Okay, 'nuff said. You don't deserve to take the heat for anything—but everyone else does. (Oh, by the way, always claim credit for everything good, and deny everything bad . . . but you knew that already, didn't you?)

❖ ❖ ❖

5

Criticize Early and Often

Always make sure to be the caustic critic. Let's face it: There isn't enough complaining in this world. There's too much Pollyanna-ish cheer and frivolity. Too many people just smile and let things go. Don't go along with them. There's something wrong with *everything and everyone* if you look closely enough, and by golly, you have to make it your job to find it first and complain about it loudest.

Let's take some easy examples: Your wife might look pretty good when she's setting out on her first day of work, but is every single, solitary hair in its place? Let her know that she doesn't look perfect enough. Don't let her get away with not looking her best. And maybe she's gained a bit of weight. Tell her that you've noticed those extra pounds. Make sure you point it all out. After all, you're just being constructive.

Your husband used up most of his Saturday mowing the lawn? Fine, but how about putting in some new plants to give the yard some color! Let him have it—why should he have any chance to relax? Get him out there working while you lounge in front of the TV. Your son did well in his last soccer game? Okay, but he missed two goals that looked easy to you. Why let him off the hook? Why let *anyone* off easy? Your daughter is doing great at gymnastics? Well, if she's so great, why didn't she get the gold medal at the last meet? She must have screwed up in some way. Let her know you that you've been paying attention, and criticize her until she sobs in frustration. That should make her do better next time.

What's the point of your being the world's most gifted observer and critic if you end up wasting all of your special talents and let people slide by?

Spare the criticism and you spoil the wife (or husband or child or employee or friend or whatever). The whole world needs to know that they're far from perfect. They can't just go about lollygagging and thinking they're doing fine. They need help—just as surely as you *don't* need it.

You're the important one, the perfect one, and people have to pay attention to what you say. The world is a crappy place anyway, right? Laying withering criticism on every situation assures that everyone knows you're in charge—and everyone is lucky that you are!

※ ※ ※

6

Never Be Grateful

And I mean never! Why should you? Think about it for a minute: You live in the richest, freest, most beautiful country in the world. Of course you have a great car and air conditioning and a comfortable place to live, but there's still lots to be angry about. I mean, isn't Bill Gates richer than you are? Isn't Ashley Judd better looking? Isn't Britney Spears more famous? Isn't Tiger Woods a better golfer? So why should you be grateful? You have a lot to be sore about.

True, a lot of sappy sentimentalists might be grateful for small favors, but you're a hard-headed realist. You can see that our whole society is going to hell in a handbasket.

Just a few examples will make the case easily: What's with music today? It's horrible, and is obviously rotting the brains of our young people. What about the obscene way teenagers dress? Yes, the kids may like it, but isn't it all really about how it affects *you*? And if *you* don't like it, what do you have to be grateful for? (And while we're at it, make sure you always think in this way: How does it affect *you*? Nothing else and no one else matters.) Remember that checkout clerk at the grocery store? Well, she practically ruined your morning with her sappy "Have a nice day." It's impossible to be grateful with such revolting behavior in your midst.

What about the environment? Yes, it might look okay where you are, but what about in the national forests out West? There's a drought, and fires galore! And right here at home, isn't your wife's cooking or your husband's woodworking lacking in the proficiency department? You bet. There's not much room for gratitude with suffering like this going on. There's plenty to moan about.

And please don't forget to feel ungrateful toward your parents. What did they ever do for you? Sure, they stayed up nights with you for years. Okay, maybe they got up early when they didn't want to so they could get you to school on time. And yes, they might have worked extra hours or even two jobs to get you the car or summer camp excursion you wanted. But that was what they *owed* you. You were their child. It should have been a pleasure and a gift to make sacrifices for you. Now, of course, you don't feel as if it's a pleasure and a gift to get up at six to get your own kid off to school. *But that's the exact point, friend! You are special and different, and people owe you in a way that you don't owe anyone else.*

So do yourself a big favor: Don't let gratitude even enter your mind. The world hasn't completely bowed down before your perfection yet, and it's very far from being a perfect place, so what's there to be grateful for? If you start feeling gratitude—even in some small way—that means you're weak, so forget it.

❖ ❖ ❖

7

Know That You're the Source of All Wisdom

The world needs your advice to run properly—not just your criticism, but your guidance. Have you noticed what a mess society is in? Horrifying terrorism at home and abroad. This wouldn't have happened if *you* had been running the FBI and the CIA, or if they'd at least called you every day for your words of wisdom. War in the Middle East? You could easily avert it if Messrs. Arafat and Sharon would just ask *you* what should be done in the Gaza Strip and Tel Aviv. Starvation in Africa? You have the solution right under your hat. But have the fools asked *you?* No, they did not. Crime in the streets? Serious spread of the AIDS virus? Religious rancor? Turmoil in the stock market and widespread financial fraud? Why? Because the world isn't getting enough of *your* advice! You know more than anyone else about finance, counterterrorism, peace among and within religions, and the control of infectious diseases.

Yes, I already mentioned criticism, but this is something different. This is about advice—not just saying "nay," but offering specific pointers. The world is in a mess because too much of its business goes on without anyone consulting you and getting your marching orders.

And it gets worse right within your circle. One friend is getting a divorce; another one is gaining weight. Still another one is losing his job and maybe his house. And one's kid can't get her schoolwork done. Why? Well, there are a lot of causes (mostly because if they ain't you, their name is *loser!*), but only one sure cure: Consult you and get *your* advice. You would most assuredly know how to solve every one of those dilemmas in a heartbeat.

Why don't they ask? Because they're jealous and not as smart as you are. But just because they don't ask, that doesn't mean you shouldn't offer your unsolicited advice. In fact, to be generous about it, you should positively insist that they heed your words of wisdom immediately, and take notes while they're at it. *You* know how to save that marriage. *You* know how to get that guy's job back, and you can certainly turn that kid into an A student.

And if your neighbors are too darned incompetent to ask, you have to get in their faces and make them know what's best for them. Don't let any minor blemishes in your own life slow you down for even one minute as far as putting in your two cents' worth is concerned. The point is that people have to learn to do as you say, not as you do. It's your duty as a god who walks the earth to make sure that everyone gets the benefit of your experience on every issue. Please don't forget it. And when you *do* give your advice, don't be stingy with it. Go into long-winded detail, and make sure they get it right by going over whatever you say over and over and over again.

※ ※ ※

8

Envy Everything; Appreciate Nothing

Envy everyone. For example, your neighbor has a better lawn. Forget the possibility that this is because he worked harder tending it, watering it, and fertilizing it. Logic plays no part here. Just the fact that he has that emerald-green lawn is reason enough for envy. The other neighbor has a Caddy while you have an old Yugo. Never mind that he worked long hours and got a second degree by going to school at night so he could get a better job. He's got a better car. That, by itself, is plenty reason to feel envy. Or how about the guy who hangs out next to you at the tavern? He just got a beautiful young girlfriend and you've been observing (and pointing out!) that your wife is getting a bit hippy. Never mind that your wife is the most loyal creature on this earth. Never mind her devotion and kindness to you over the decades. Just forget about that stuff. In fact, forget about everything in your life that's good. *Only concentrate on what you don't have that other people do.*

That mother's kid got into Harvard. So what if she worked with him for hours on his papers and extracurricular activities while you snoozed. The kid is still getting into Harvard, while yours will be lucky to graduate from high school. Plenty of reason to feel envy. Especially since, as we know, if somebody isn't you, he's a loser by definition.

That one's wife has a better figure than yours. Of course she's also always in a bad mood from dieting, and she never has a nice word to say, but she *does* have a good build, so there's reason to feel still more envy. That one's husband has a more lucrative job than yours. Hey, come to think of it, when you start, there's almost everything to envy and almost nada to be happy about. Just make your way down the road to envy and you won't ever return. You'll just get more and more envious until you disappear right up your own exhaust.

Envy is a perfect poison. Taken regularly throughout the day, it can ruin anything decent going on in your life. Therefore . . . don't forget to take it in good measure minute by minute! It can turn a sunny day cloudy, and get your juices flowing when you're calm. It's sort of the ultimate way to make sure that you and everyone around you are attached to the electrical grid of high tension every second. I think if I were to tell you the one sure way to jam the gears of everyone anywhere near you, it would be to embrace envy. In fact, if you have enough envy, you don't even need poison.

❀ ❀ ❀

9

Be a Perfectionist

In your life, everything and everyone has to be perfect. Don't be satisfied with yourself or anyone else unless what you do is absolutely impeccable. Don't just do it well enough to get by; torture yourself until it's perfect, and torture everyone around you, too. In fact, keep in your mind the powerful injunction that *everything* you do has to be perfect. And then you'll be so paralyzed with inaction that you won't do anything at all for fear that it won't turn out just right.

For example, your husband suggests that you learn how to garden so you can spruce up the outdoor area. Sure, it might not be a bad idea (although let's remember that only *you* truly have good ideas, not anyone else). But could your roses ever compare with those at the gardens at Versailles, or the White House? Probably not. Then why bother to even try? Or maybe you think you should write a letter of sympathy to someone who's lost a parent. Well, for one thing, the world revolves around *you*, not anyone else. But also, and this is very important, your note might not be as good as Shakespeare could have crafted it. So why do it at all?

This one is a jewel. Just tell yourself before you buy a computer that you simply have to get the best buy on the Internet—and watch, you won't end up purchasing anything at all. If you're going to get a new car, you have to get the best bargain anyone has ever gotten in the history of car buying—otherwise, you ain't plunking down that check. If you plan to write a paper, make sure it's going to be the best one since the Gettysburg Address. But you know it won't be that good, so why not just blow it off?

You get the picture, you genius, you! If you handle your life in just this way, you'll soon do nothing at all unless it's perfect, and since that might not turn out to be the case, well . . . next thing you know, you will simply, again, do zero.

◈ ◈ ◈

10

Think Too Big

Set enormous, unattainable goals. Don't just be content to teach your son how to cast a fishing line on a sunny Sunday morning. Instead, seclude yourself and plan to create a company out of your garage that will be bigger than Microsoft. And then take a nap. Or have a drink.

Here's another: Instead of simply enjoying the afternoon breeze while you help your husband clear the leaves from the lawn, read in the financial magazines about people who have made billions selling T-shirts from the back of their car. Then make plans to be even bigger and richer than they are, and completely avoid enjoying the loveliness of the moment. Don't just do what's in front of you, like your work at the office or your shopping or your schoolwork. No, that's far too puny for you. You're a world beater, a conqueror. The small achievements and enjoyments of life are far too trivial for you. When you think about a task, make it so elaborate and complex that it never gets completed.

And this is closely connected to the next piece of guidance . . .

11

Don't Enjoy the Simple Things in Life

Ignore life's little pleasures. Don't take pleasure in a child's smile. Don't enjoy a sunset. Don't take pleasure out of a simple but well-cooked meal. For you, things have to be elaborate, intricate, and incomprehensibly grand to make any sense. So just gloss over a friendly smile from a clerk or a pat on the back from a friend. Go for the big stuff. And if you can't get it, be miserable about the fact that the world has cheated its only deity . . . again.

12

Fix Anyone and Everyone at Any Time

This is a big one, so take notes:

Form relationships with people who have lots of problems, and believe in your heart you can *change them.* Yes, this is perhaps the supreme piece of advice, so please don't forget it: *Believe in your heart that you can do the impossible—change and fix people.*

Marry the guy who can't keep a job and drinks too much every day and night. Then, tell him sharply that you want him to stay sober, get a good job, and keep it. Nag him and badger him and throw out his liquor, and cry when he goes to the bar. Pretty soon, you'll have him stone-cold sober. Yup, just for you, he'll do it, what no man has ever done before—stay sober as a result of a woman's nagging.

Or, move in with that woman who's broken every heart she's ever touched with her two-timing treachery. Tell her you expect her to be perfectly faithful, and for you, she'll stay on the straight and narrow. If you do catch her cheating, throw a fit and maybe throw away her favorite CDs—next thing you know, she'll purr like a kitten for you and only you.

Yes, you'll hear over and over again that people can't be changed, but that doesn't apply to you! You alone will be the very first human being ever to mold others to your desires. You can succeed where everyone else has failed. Human character may be totally immutable to most people—but not to you! And don't give up trying until you actually do make that change. It's just around the corner. That employee of yours who fakes being sick and sits around all day wasting company money? Sure, he'll change. The business partner who's a habitual liar and takes money from the cash drawer? Speak plainly but sharply, and you'll get the changes you want and deserve.

It used to be believed that years of brainwashing in a North Korean torture camp plus mind-altering drugs were the only techniques that could make a person change, and then not for long. But for you, it's all different.

People really do change—*but only for you.*

❀ ❀ ❀

13

Treat the People who Are Good to You Badly

Who cares if they're good to you? They're your doormats—they exist solely for you to trample upon. They have nothing to say to you that's worth hearing. Basically, they're your servants. No, slaves. And they'll always be good to you because they sense that you're superior to them—and they're right. They know that you're a deity, and they're just insignificant pebbles on the bottom of the sea of life. Yes, you, of course, have the most intense and exquisite feelings. But no one else has emotions that need be taken into account.

Just use them and abuse them and toss them away when you feel like it. Imagine how the Aztec gods treated their worshipers—causing them to be sacrificed and to have their hearts ripped out while still breathing. That's how you should treat the people who are good to you—although you can skip the drama.

If someone at your job is loyal to you, often stays late to get projects done, and then eventually needs your support to get a raise, tell him he's on his own. If you have a teacher who's patient with you and helps you learn something—as if you weren't born knowing it all!—don't thank her—just walk right past her on the last day of school without saying a word. If you have a friend who's listened to you when you continually bemoaned a lost love, don't even answer the phone when she calls to ask you for a favor.

Biting the hand that feeds you is one of the absolutely surest, most skillfully crafted weapons you possess. But then you already knew that, because (now I'm preaching to the choir!) you know *everything*.

Just in case you haven't committed it to memory, though, remember it now: You don't owe anyone a darned thing, and the people who are nice to you . . . well, they're just suckers and losers anyway. They're beaten-down curs that you can treat any way you please. And that old saw about treating people nicely and the Golden Rule and all that garbage . . . hey, those are just old wives' tales from a very old Book. Just forget about it. You know very well that you don't get to be rich and famous being considerate to others. It's *their* job to treat *you* well, and it's your absolute right to treat them like dirt.

❖ ❖ ❖

14

Treat the People who Are Bad to You well

That's right. They'll soon change and start being really, really good to you. Maybe. But whether they do or not, let's be honest about this: Some weird urge in you tells you to knuckle under and treat the people who are bad to you *really* well. In some way you can't quite explain right now, the people who treat you like dirt will greatly enrich your life somewhere down the road if you just treat them really nicely—preferably ignoring those who were good to you in the process.

The gal who two-timed you when you were madly in love with her? Buy her jewelry. The agent who promised he'd get your deal done and then slept on the job? Forget about it. He'll be really useful to you someday, so give him a flat-screen color TV. Treating the real creeps in your life well gives you a lot of satisfaction and is actually a stress reliever. So keep doing it. It will pay off immensely, in the way that allowing yourself to be dumped on by bad people always does!

This is a mystery, but it's a good mystery: When you treat the people who show you contempt with nothing but respect . . . you'll find that you'll end up being a happy guy or doll. Someday.

❀ ❀ ❀

15

Hang Out with the Wrong Crowd

Associate with unlucky, unsuccessful people with revolting habits on a regular basis. Yes, no matter how bad your life seems, there will always be those who are drunker, have saved less money, have incurred more debts, have gotten into more trouble with the law, and are lonelier than you are. Make these people your pals. It will make you feel better to be around such sad sacks. You can feel superior all of the time. And their bad habits will never rub off on you, because you're perfect—even if the world at large doesn't know it yet. From now on, when you feel bad, you've got human support levels under you in the form of people who are worse off than you.

It's especially useful to hang around people who abuse drugs or alcohol or lie a lot or brag all of the time. And it's really a great idea to interact with individuals who are pretentious and boast without having a thing to brag about. And associating with people who never tell the truth will always pay off big. Plus, it's nice to be around people with no money, bad breath, dirty hair, and unkempt clothes. It's really top drawer if they reek of body odor as well.

These annoying habits will never ever stick to you, though. No, sir. No, ma'am. Instead, you'll become more and more successful just by associating with such a stellar crowd. You may have heard that others will be judged by their friends. *But not you.* No one can judge you because you're the supreme judge of humankind. Not only that, but you're so unique that no one will ever be in a position to adequately gauge your greatness, just as no one can look into a bright sun for more than a few moments . . .

So keep those human dregs around you, and see how much happier you'll be!

❀ ❀ ❀

16

Make the People Around You Feel Small

That's it. Make 'em squirm. Belittle them on a regular basis, and brag as much as you can about your family, your job, your car, and the people you know. If your next-door neighbor has lost a bundle in the stock market, tell him how much money you just made with your own investments. If the poor guy looks crestfallen, tell him that you wouldn't have made the mistakes he's made in a million years. If the woman in the next cubicle just broke up with her boyfriend, tell her how long you've been happily married.

If your secretary tells you that her car keeps breaking down, make a point of reminding her that your car never has any problems and is always in great shape. Don't disguise the scorn you feel for her—how stupid could she have been to buy such a crummy car in the first place?!

You can accomplish all of this really skillfully, too. Stick the knife in when your colleague is really down and depressed. Do it especially when it has to do with money. This one can really hurt. Just run wild with your boasting. Brag as much as you can about everything in your life. (But again, concentrate on money, which can really turn the screws.) Some might think that this will make the people around you despise you. But you know better (and anyway, who cares, since you're a walking godhead and everyone else is just there to worship you). Acting in this manner may actually make everybody else really look up to you and even worship you. They want to be insulted and humiliated—maybe not by anyone else—but by *you*, sure! In fact, it's a privilege for them to have you lord it over them . . . and they'd better learn to like it!

❀ ❀ ❀

17

Keep Score

Keep a running tally of life's injustices, and get really angry about every single one of them. Yes, we all know that the world isn't meant to be fair—except where *you're* concerned! (And in that case, it's supposed to be *more* than fair.) But again, don't even think about whether it's equitable for anyone else. Your justifiable anger over anything that's not perfect for *you* is all that counts.

Don't think about the undeniable fact that there are small children in cancer wards. What matters is that the waiter at your juice bar was rude to you. It's none of your concern that people are being sold into slavery in the Sudan right now—hey, the lettuce in your salad isn't crisp enough! And what about that guy who did so much better than you in school? He must have cheated. And how come your house didn't go up in value as much as your sister's? You've been robbed, my friend, and we both know it. Yes, it's a beautiful day, and you're feeling healthy, but what about the bum advice your stockbroker gave you last month? You wuz robbed! This is more than envy. This is about letting the universe know that you're owed a better deal. Get furious and hold on to that anger, as well as that feeling of being cheated. That will most assuredly help you get through your day really steamed, which is a lot more interesting than just feeling cool and collected.

When you feel as if you might be having a great day, recall some real or imagined slight that someone inflicted upon you. Remember when your friend insisted on sitting in the front seat of the car that time you were on a double date? Or think about a stock you bought that went up right after you sold it. Maybe you can recall someone who cut ahead of you in line at the airport ten years ago. And what about that old college friend who's ended up being so much more successful than you?

Let's get serious. There's nothing to be happy about when you start to carefully ponder every possible thing to be *miserable* about. Surprise!—you'll find that the list is almost endless. Just continue keeping score, and you'll find that you're always losing. And keep that anger burning red hot, churning up your stomach, preventing you from sleeping, and keeping you from appreciating the beauty around you. Anger is its own reward, and so is feeling perpetually cheated.

※ ※ ※

18

Use Drugs
and Alcohol Freely

This is another huge one:

Tune in, turn on, and wreck your life. True, you may have heard that there's no human so powerful or lofty that drugs and alcohol can't bring that creature to the gutter. Yes, drug and alcohol abuse can wreck the lives of superstars and billionaires. Every entertainment magazine is full of stories of men and women who were on top of the world and were brought to their knees by poverty, insanity, and premature death by overuse of drugs and alcohol. Since you're a special genius, you know that the mental hospitals of this country are loaded with men and women who got there by being high and staying high. You've probably known family members who ruined their lives (and their family's lives as well) as a result of drug and alcohol addiction. Yes, drugs and alcohol used to excess are deadly poisons for most people.

But you're different. You can drink day after day and not get dependent on it. Truth is, you're funnier, sharper, better looking, and more confident with a little booze in you. It brings out your natural sophistication and wit. You get to be like one of those lively, charismatic characters you see in films, like James Bond—"shaken, not stirred," ha ha. Nah, alcohol is no problem for you. You've tried it and you like it, but you can quit any time. In fact, you've quit two dozen times. Sure, the sauce makes you argue with your spouse and neglect your kids. But you know what? If liquor was so bad, why would it be sold on every street corner? Why would you see people on TV every day merrily belting it down? And if a celebrity can handle it, you can, too, my mighty friend.

Now what about those drugs? The reefer, the weed, the Ecstasy, the pills? Well, what the heck were they invented for? I mean, life stinks when the world doesn't recognize your greatness, and it's really only bearable when you're high on something. You'll never become an addict like those other losers, and all of those warnings are just scare tactics for punks.

Look, half the doctors in America are high on prescription drugs right now. You know it for a fact. You read it somewhere. Or maybe someone told you at your office. And the drug companies make billions peddling the stuff—and they're big, respectable public corporations. So how bad can drugs be? I mean, if you can get a doctor to write a scrip for a drug that calms you down or gives you a little buzz, why can't you just forego that visit to the medical building? And why not just skip the whole medical establishment route and simply call your pal from college and buy a lid? Or a gram or two? It's not just that it makes you feel better. It's *cool*. The coolest people in films do it. The coolest kids at your school do it. Why shouldn't you do something that makes you feel good and is also distinctly hip?

That stuff about one drug leading to a stronger one doesn't apply to a man or woman with your willpower. You're far too strong to even consider getting dependent on marijuana and then needing something stronger like heroin to get through the day. True, you've found it pretty rocky sledding when you did try to get through a day without your drugs, but if it were really important, you could just chuck 'em any old time. Let's remember: You're the boss. The drugs work for you. You own them. They don't own you—and no matter what they've done to other people, drugs will never control *you.*

So, when you want to start feeling a little better, don't hesitate to take out the bottle or the pills. You deserve a break today—and every day. It's your God-given right to avoid ever feeling any emotion you don't want to feel. So if drugs and alcohol do it for you (and why shouldn't they?), hey, go for it!

◈ ◈ ◈

19

Don't Save Any Money

Repeat after me: "I don't need no stinkin' savings!" Thrift? That's for fraidy cats and nerds. You're always going to have a great job or score big on the stock market or have "friends" you can take advantage of. Money will be like low-hanging fruit on trees all around you. There won't be any rainy days in *your* life. Money will just pour in by magic. Plus, in the remote event that your money flow slows down a bit, you have a special flexibility that no one else has. You can live just as well spending a little or a lot. Many people have problems adjusting to having less money to spend. But not you. You can live on a million dollars a year or on nothing flat. You're like a Buddhist holy man. You're far above the petty gravity of money. So, it doesn't matter if you have money saved. You are you, indestructible and defiant.

Plus, let's think about it for second. Savings are for people who don't know how to enjoy life in the moment. But *you* have a special sense of how to appreciate life. You like to spend money when you feel good—*and when you feel bad*—you dog, you. You know precisely how to use your cash when you want something and not hold back. The people who cheat themselves by not spending when they should be enjoying themselves? Losers! Something ～～～ ～ver be. You're a champagne-and-cavia～ ～vidual, and if others aren't, that's th～

I ～ ～ike you're ever going to get old a～ ～d still need money to live on. You～ ～ ～ever lose your job and have to～ ～ ～p worrying about paying your ～ ～n't ever need the down payment ～ ～from it. No, it'll always be smooth ～ ～cloudless sky. The money will just keep ～～～ ～, in. Recessions and layoffs are words in someone else's vocabulary, not yours.

And if you do hit a rough patch, you can always scare up some loser who did save, and scrounge money from him. Why do you think the Almighty made savers and little insignificant people who squirrel away money? So that they can be around to lend (really, *give*) you money. True, you may have heard that "neither a lender nor a borrower" should you be. But that doesn't apply to you, friend. In fact, it's a privilege to lend to someone as great as you. Many people go through life just saving, saving, saving. *Boring!* And what good does it do them? It might as well be donkey dung. No, the only way it would do them any good is if they used it to get closer to a sweetheart like you. So do them a favor: Don't save, and let them have the chance to lend you money down the road.

You ask, "What if they won't lend me money when I'm in need?" Honey, that's not possible. Not for a doll like you. What if it rains bananas? Don't save, and you'll be fascinated by what happens if you need money suddenly. It won't just be your genial next-door neighbor or your ex-wife or your long-lost cousins who rush to help you out. No, far from it. It will be the "Big Boys": Credit card firms, auto loan companies, banks, insurance agencies— all of them will happily postpone your payments indefinitely if you just give them a handshake and a smile. No, of course they don't do that for just anyone. But for you, life without money will be a breeze. Friends, creditors—basically everyone in your life—has a secret wish to accommodate you when you're a little short in the bread drawer. Just spend and spend and let the money run out, and you'll be pleasantly surprised by how easy life is without any funds.

Money is like drugs and alcohol to you: You can do great with it or great without it. You're in charge.

◈ ◈ ◈

20

🔶 🔶 🔶 🔶 🔶 🔶

Ignore Your Family

Get rid of those balls and chains. This is contrary to what you may have heard from other folks, but it's true, nonetheless—at least for you! Family? They're just a burden on you anyway. Who needs 'em? Sure, they're there for you whenever you need companionship and support (as if a superhero like you needed such trivialities—ha!). That's right, when the rest of the world has forgotten you, they're there. So freaking what? You have to be a rolling stone, a freewheeling guy with no attachments, Jack Nicholson in *Easy Rider.* You have to be Marlon Brando in *The Wild One,* and Keanu Reeves in *The Matrix.* You have to be free to act out your dreams and fantasies. A family only slows you down.

Of course you want them around when they can do something for you, but when they need *you*, the hell with 'em. Responsibilities such as paying bills and helping to cook dinner? Forget it. When did James Bond have to pay utility bills or help with the algebra homework? No, that's not for a secret agent/playboy/rock star like you. You think Dirty Harry had stacks of bills to pay? Or spelling lists to help his kid with? No way. Look, you might condescend to be there when your son scores the winning goal. You'll show up if your daughter is elected homecoming queen, sure. But if they have problems, it'll do 'em good to work them out by themselves. That's how character gets built. Just ignore your kids when they need you, and see how big and strong they grow up to be. (And how happy and proud *you'll* be if you know in your heart that you ignored them when they were young.)

Yes, I know. When you ignore them, it's not always pretty. They may cry or look hurt, but that's just part of growing up. If they were as smart as you are (and who is?) the kids would know that you're doing them a huge favor by forcing them to make it on their own. I mean, teenagers are always whining that they want to be left alone. Well, here's their chance. You'll be off living it up and saving the universe and sleeping late. In the end, both you and the kids will be a lot better off.

Your parents? Screw 'em. They're boring, and what the heck did they ever do besides nag you? In fact, their behavior is usually outrageous, practically unforgivable. They tell you, mighty *you*, what to do. You! That's right. They tell you to eat right, to get enough sleep, to save your money, to be careful. Can you believe that? That's like telling a river how to flow or the stars how to shine.

Maybe they did some things for you when you were a child. Maybe they fed you and sheltered you and cleaned up your poop. Maybe they were patient with you when no one else would be. Maybe they were in your corner when you would have been alone. So what? That was what they were supposed to do. How many times do they have to get the message? They did their job, and now it's time to move on to bigger and better things.

And by the way, in the extremely unlikely event that anyone would say there's anything wrong with you, it's your parents who screwed you up. Let's not forget that. Those old folks who try to look so sweet and innocent and harmless? By every psychiatric theory, parents are to blame for everything. So if you're a bit selfish sometimes and don't always remember every single little detail of what you're "supposed" to do, whose fault is that? *Right-o—their* fault, and no one else's. So, forget 'em, I say. They're lucky that you don't report them to someone—even now when you're 30 or 40. And if you find yourself feeling lonely without them, just have a drink. Or buy something.

Your spouse keeps demanding your attention when you should be getting it all? And he/she expects you to actually do things around the house? I mean, what are wives and husbands for? To look good and be available for sex in the event you feel like having it, that's what! After that, they might as well be prison guards. If they're just gonna tell you what to do, who needs 'em? A mate should just be there when you want something, and then be still and silent the rest of the time—like a comfy chair. If wifey or hubby can't do that, just get 'em the hell out of your life.

Family is highly overrated. You'll do great without them. And really, they'll be better off, too. The world is such a warm, friendly place that it just makes sense for people to be out in it as individuals, not with anyone on their team—especially not if it means any real effort by you. Just ditch your family . . . but by all means, do expect them to be there for you if you need help on the spur of the moment!

※ ※ ※

21

Know That the Rules of Reasonable, Decent Conduct Don't Apply to You

Rise above it all.

Let me give you a few examples—as if you needed them:

Income taxes: They're a major pain in the butt to figure out. You have to collect all kinds of documents, go through them, sort them, make notes, and then you often have to shell out some cash. Sometimes a lot of cash. Well, only idiots pay their full income taxes. (Don't you recall that fine example of a noble life, Leona Helmsley, saying that ". . . only little people pay taxes"? Learn from her, you big, lovable lug.) In fact, why bother to submit a return at all? It's a ton of work, and hey, there are hundreds of millions of other people filing their returns. What the heck does the IRS need one more for? The employees at the IRS are just ordinary working schmoes like you. Why burden them with extra paper?

And if and when you do file and do it wrong, don't worry. The IRS will never catch you. If they do, they'll just chuckle and tell you to please not do it again. Everyone knows that the IRS is good-natured and sweet and easy to get along with. Have you ever had an audit? Then you know very well what great people they are. They love a good laugh, especially at their own expense. They're just a bunch of bureaucrats who want to hang around the water cooler all day telling dirty jokes. Save them a little work, and save yourself a lot, and see how grateful the IRS folks are. (Again, if you do file, don't even think of paying what you actually owe. Just pay what you feel like. It's enough of a pain in the butt to pay anything at all as it is. You've got to leave *some* for yourself. Let the other poor slobs pick up the slack.)

Driving: Hey, pal, you own the road. Drive any old way you please. Only geeks go the speed limit. You're in a hurry. And besides, you were born knowing how to be a racecar driver. Those speed limits apply to little old ladies and wimps. You could drive 80 anywhere in any city or on any highway with your eyes closed—and sometimes I'll bet you do, you rascal!—and never have a problem. The least a true Indy-class driver like you can do is drive at any speed you find comfortable.

Buckle up your safety belts? Why? You're not going to crash, and hey, the belt makes your shoulder itch. Besides, you read somewhere that it's better not to wear your safety belt because you can get trapped in your car when you need to get out in an emergency—like to have a drink or buy something.

Signal when changing lanes? What for? That's someone else's problem, not yours. Tune up your car and get your brakes checked? You would if you had time, but you're busy. Let the other people on the road worry about *you.* You don't have the time right now to worry about *them.* Anyway, you're never going to have an accident. I mean, you've never even gotten a ticket, right?

Smoking: Hey, you're not a baby. You can do what you want. So what if there's a mountain of data that warns that smoking can kill you or give you cancer that eats away at your tongue and liver and lungs? Didn't you just see a WWII movie with John Wayne where all those guys were smoking? And weren't they as tough as old boots? Sure they were. Remember how The Duke kicked all that Nazi ass? Not only that, but in every gangster movie, those guys are smoking. So why can't you? And didn't you meet some guy who told you that his uncle smoked all his life and lived to be 88? Hey, George Burns smoked lots of cigars and lived to be 100! Plus, smoking makes you feel good. Just one drag, and that rich, lovely nicotine is all over your lungs and blood making you feel safe and secure. Take a deep puff and watch a third of the cigarette turn to ash that goes right to your immortal cardiopulmonary system. Enjoy yourself!

Planning for the future: No way. You're a happy-go-lucky guy or doll. You need to enjoy the moment. It takes too much brainpower to think beyond this very moment. It creates furrows in your forehead, so why the heck bother? Actually write down some plans and some numbers and try to live within them? Uh, I don't think so. I believe that spells "N-E-R-D," and that ain't you. Did you ever see James Dean making little budgets or plans on a sheet of yellow legal paper? Did you ever see Clint Eastwood doing it or Tom Cruise? What about Liz Taylor or Julia Roberts? Then why would *you* do it? Do you think that a living, breathing deity has to make dopey little plans? No, *you* control the future, so why should you have to worry about it? The future will be whatever you want it to be.

Home ownership: Buy a house so you won't be paying rent all of your life? That's too much hassle. It's a lot of work to fill out all of those mortgage forms. Plus, you have to shop around and pack up and move. But hey, maybe a good fairy will just magically move you to a house. Anyway, this all comes under the heading of worrying about the future, and that's a big no-no. You already know this, but . . . the future will take care of itself. You don't have to do a darned thing you don't want to do.

Being reliable: Return things you borrow? Why? They're *your* things now! Besides, who cares? There will always be another sucker to give you whatever you need. Return *money* you borrow? I don't think so! I mean, what on earth is the point of borrowing money if you have to pay it back?

What good does that do you? You'd just be in the same position you were in before if every asset was also a liability. For royalty like you, there's really no such concept as "borrow." There's "give," as in "gimme"; and "take," as in "I'll take that." Those are the only options, and by God, we know who the taker is in this world. It's you, you, you. I want to emphasize this again. Why borrow if you just have to repay? No, don't even think about it.

Hygiene: Oh, here's a good one: Don't bother to keep yourself neat and clean. Of course you can't stand the smell of body odor and bad breath and stale cigarettes and whiskey on others. It's disgusting. But when it emanates from you, it smells like the finest French perfume. You have the right to expect others to be fresh as a daisy, but *you* don't have to be. That's not in your job description, any more than it's expected that babies or Greek gods would have to dress themselves and keep themselves spic and span. You can look any old way you want, and people will be happy to have you around, period.

Yup, when it comes to any of the above situations, you can do whatever the heck you feel like—but you get to complain and criticize every other person on earth for any old reason you want! And that's what rising above it all is all about!

22

Live As If Truth Is Relative—a Distant Relative

Don't tell the truth if you don't feel like it. The "truth" is just a way to hem you in, control you, and tie you up in knots when you have to "confess" to things that might seem a little embarrassing to you. The real truth, the one that matters, is whatever works for you and saves your behind. There's no objective truth except what's good for you, sister. And who cares if you get caught lying? That's someone else's problem.

No one else can judge you. Only *you* can judge you. I think Charlie Manson once said that, didn't he?

Truth, like paying taxes, might be a factor for the little person, but it doesn't exist for you. Truth is a lovely thing for poets and philosophers to talk about, but it doesn't mean a thing to you if it gets in your way. I mean, think about it like this: Great nations often tell fibs in diplomatic situations. They say they won't attack and then they do. They say some dude wasn't a spy when he was. If nations can do that, why can't you? You're at least as important as any country that ever existed, aren't you?

And by the way, last time I looked, you weren't a prisoner in some damned Commie country. You don't have to confess to anything. You're allowed under the Constitution to lie all you want. Don't politicians do it? Don't business owners do it? Don't they do it in advertisements for hair-replacement products and stuff like that all of the time? Then why can't *you* do it? Why on earth, in a world where lying is commonplace, should you ever have to tell the truth? And so what if you betray people's trust? That's their problem. You aren't the freaking tooth fairy or whoever's in charge of the truth. You are you—a living, breathing deity—and the truth is just dirt under your gilded feet.

On the other hand, if telling the truth advances your cause, then everyone else has to be bound by it, too.

Maybe I can make this even more clear: All concepts and principles exist for you to either use or ignore, depending on whether they help you or not. If it doesn't help you, it's bogus; and if it does help you, it's great. It's that simple, because, hey, you're at the center of the universe, with all of creation revolving slowly around you.

※ ※ ※

23

Remember That No One Else Counts

Always remember that relationships are worthless. Now, you may have heard a silly rumor that relationships are vital and that the most important book you'll ever own is your own Rolodex. And you may also have heard that you have to be good to people because you might need them someday.

This is nonsense. You know better. You can and must treat people any old way you want. You don't ever need to think about doing favors for others or being good to them so they'll remember you and be there to help you get a job or get your child into school. People will always want to do whatever you want them to do *at the exact moment* you want them to. No matter how you treat them, they'll be right at your beck and call. Ordinary people aren't even going to remember whether you helped them when they needed something. They won't hold a grudge if you treated them poorly. Far from it. No, instead, they'll very much want to assist you in any possible way. In fact, you can treat all of the people you know like dirt (or, like the lowly mortals they are) and they'll still want to help you at any time.

Let me give you an example. You have a desire to get a job in show business, and you happen to have a cousin who works in the entertainment industry. Well, don't bother showing him any kindness or courtesy. Borrow things and don't return them. Make fun of him. Bait him on his political and religious beliefs . . . because you know that even then, he'll be perfectly happy to do whatever he can for you!

Or suppose you have a relative who's a doctor. She could help you deal with that persistent cough you've had for about 15 years (gee, could smoking have anything to do with it?). Maybe she might even know a painless way to get you off tobacco.

So, the thing to do is . . . don't remember her birthday. Don't lift a finger for her. Don't inquire about her children or her husband. Just treat them all like dirt . . . and they'll be ready to help you anyway. Remember how I told you that it's best to treat the people who are good to you badly and treat the people who are bad to you well? This is just another example.

Besides, why would a guy or gal like you ever need any kind of help anyway? Did Zeus need any help? Did the archangels of the Lord? No, and neither do you. You came from the womb perfect, without any need for human companionship or assistance. Relationships are just baggage, like family. And if you do need people at some time, they'll be ready to help just because you're you. That's more than enough reason. This may seem to be a bit similar to some other rules about mistreating other people, and maybe it is. But I need to reiterate it to remind you that you can't ever place too low a value on human relationships.

※ ※ ※

24

Know That You Don't Owe Anyone a Thing

Hold this thought: Obligations are for suckers. The universe was made for your enjoyment, not for you to do anything for anyone else. Your boss wants something from you? Too bad. Why would that jerk think you owe him a thing just because he pays you a salary? What a freaking money-grubbing creep! You're owed that money just for being there or really, just for existing. You don't have to do a damned thing for it.

Your spouse expects you to be somewhere to help with a project? The heck with it. You have your own plans. (Remember, families are worth-less.) You're not anyone's slave. You have a right to do whatever you feel like doing anytime you want. Why would anyone think that he or she owns you? Didn't I already explain how the 13th Amendment ended slavery? Well, just lay it out for whoever's asking: You have your own needs and plans and wishes. You don't owe anyone else a damned thing!

Some old biddy who was a pal of your mom's wants something from you? Maybe she's the same woman who got your mother a job to help her pay her way through college? Hey, is that ancient his-tory or what? Who the heck cares? It was long ago and far away, and that's all there is to it. I mean, you have important things to do today—like that big football game you want to watch on TV. Just forget all about any sense of obligation to anyone.

This country? Someone actually expects you to be grateful for the soldiers who fought and died to keep this country free? Why? Fuggetabout it. You didn't know any of those people, did you? That all happened a long time before you were even born. They didn't know you. They didn't do it for you. They did it because they enjoyed freezing in France and getting their arms and legs blown off while they were starving. They did it because they had nothing better to do. They wanted to land on red sand in Iwo Jima and have a Japanese land mine blow them and their friends into little pieces. They were crazy. Besides, they got paid, didn't they? So why are they all over your case about it? It's their problem if they happened to get in the way of a bullet or a shell. It's over and done with anyway. You don't owe them nuttin'. The men and women fighting and dying in Afghanistan? Hey, that's a long ways away.

And the teachers who taught you in school? Weren't they just royal pains in the butt? They kept you from getting your much-needed sleep. You still despise them. Some of them gave you bad marks because you didn't turn in your homework—as if a creature of shining immortality like you ever had to do anything after school except hang out with your friends or watch TV. They failed you when you didn't know any answers on a test. Well, duh! Where did they get the idea that you had nothing better to do than study?

Teachers have no sense of duty or love of children. You know that, even if a lot of suckers don't. You're well aware that teachers are just in it for the big fat paycheck. They may fool the old folks, but they don't fool you, do they? No way are you going to show any respect for a bunch of losers who *teach* because they can't actually *do* anything.

And that's the bottom line: The world expects you to be grateful to a whole lot of people and institutions, and that's so darned wrong.

Everyone else should be grateful to *you!* I could go on about this, but a genius like you knows it the moment you read it: You don't owe anyone else a thing.

※ ※ ※

25

Gamble with Money

Roll dem bones! Think about it logically. You already know you're the luckiest person who ever walked the earth. So why not make it official and actually lay down some bucks to prove just how lucky you are? True, Las Vegas and Atlantic City exist mostly because the gambler usually loses. But you know very well that the ordinary rules of life don't apply to you. The little ordinary gambler or even the high roller is a loser if only for one huge reason: He's not you! You're perfect! How could the heavens allow someone as impeccable as you to lose at anything? Maybe you might lose for a few minutes or hours or even years. But over long periods of time, you'll surely be a huge winner at cards or races or sports. I mean, you're the winner of winners already, right? So why not make some big money at it?

And let's make this très simple, messieurs et madames: It's a fact that other people get their lives ruined by gambling and wind up impoverishing their families and themselves. Not only that, but it's quite rare to find someone who's been a long-term winner in gambling. But what difference does that make to *you?* You're not susceptible to what happens to the usual clod. You'll win and become fabulously rich. You're the one and only gambler in human history who will, at the end of the day, wind up in the black.

And, in fact, this amazing talent of yours is going to pull you through to glorious victory even when your friends are stumbling and suffering terribly in their puny efforts at little things such as work and saving. You'll watch them sweat and toil, but it won't matter a bit to you, because you're above the fray, tossing out chips that bring you mountains of moolah.

And don't confine your gambling to the roulette wheel or the craps table. No, no, no. Gamble with speculative stocks. Gamble with commodities futures. Gamble with incredibly complex options you don't understand. They were invented so that very lucky men and women like you could make some real dough. Plunge right in! Plunk down your money and get ready for a ride to the moon!

(Hey! Don't forget to wager on sporting events, especially those you don't know much about. Your intuition is so acute that just *hearing* the names of the teams is enough to make you a winnah!)

So go ahead. Gamble. Live it up. And don't stop gambling just because you lose the first dozen or thousand times. Keep it up, friend. And be prepared for the glorious life that awaits you.

❦ ❦ ❦

26

Make It Clear: Pets Are for Losers

Always keep in mind that pets are a pain in the ass. Now, you may have heard that a sweet little cat can keep you company and cheer you up in the worst of times. Or, that a big, warm, furry doggy can help you feel safe and peaceful when you have a string of terrible days. You may have friends (if you *have* any friends) who have told you that they owe their lives to dogs and cats who have kept them going when all else seemed lost. And you've probably heard that old chestnut about a dog being man's (and woman's) best friend.

Maybe so . . . for the weak and the meek. But you never have bad days. And you never feel weak or alone. You're all-powerful all the time. In the meantime, that darned dog or cat has to be fed, and you have to clean up the animal poopie! This is insane. Men and women at your level don't do such things, period. You do what you feel like doing, and that means that you don't clean up after anyone. (You don't even clean up after yourself, by the way, so why the heck would you clean up after a creature who can't help pay the mortgage or even read a book? Not that you read much anyway . . .)

Plus, dogs are always sniffing around and getting too close to you. The Roman emperors forbade anyone to touch them, except at their command. Similarly, any furry creature who would dare to touch *you* should be reviled. And dogs and cats need care. I've said it before and I'll say it again: You're not in the business of giving care. You're in the business of being worshiped without any reciprocal obligation.

So, let the weaklings have pets. You don't need the stinkin' hassle.

◈ ◈ ◈

27

Don't Clean
Up After Yourself

Throw away the apron. I know I've mentioned it before, but it's worth repeating: *You're a perfect being whom others are supposed to clean up after.* Just leave your dirty dishes and pots and pans lying around the house. Someone will clean it all up, even if you live alone. Leave your dirty clothes on the floor. That's not your job. You aren't a day worker in a plantation house. You have things to do, worlds to conquer. Look, you've seen *Star Wars.* Did Luke Skywalker or Han Solo go around doing laundry and folding clothes after ironing? Did either one of them clean the floors after Chewbacca had an accident? Now it's true that in *Gone with the Wind*, Scarlett did lower herself to do some cleaning. But that was only meant to show you how bad things had gotten. When things got better, she had servants to do the dirty work for her.

So freaking what if people complain that you're a slob? You don't live to please others (and there's another gem of truth for you!). You live to please *yourself*, plain and simple. (And other people live to please you!) So, get down and boogie, and let somebody else clean it all up. And if it gets too awful where you live because it's starting to look and smell like a pigsty, just move somewhere else (but make sure you leave your place a complete mess for the next tenant).

This also applies to emotional and financial messes. So what if you promised to love a man and he gave up his job and moved across the country to be near you? If you get tired of him, just cut him off without even a phone call. So what if you encouraged your partner to borrow money to start a business you were going to work with him on? If you changed your mind, that's his problem. You don't have to clean up the messes you've made. That's for the little people.

Your job in life is to please yourself moment by moment. I don't think that includes going around with a mop or a dustpan, whether real or figurative. Make any mess you want, and then go merrily on your way. It's your right.

※ ※ ※

28

Have No Respect for Age or Experience

Respect gray hair? Why should you? You were born knowing everything. And you were especially born knowing that respect for elders is a waste of time. This goes back to the concept that the best way to do anything is *your* way. Tradition? That's nonsense. Skill based on years of practice? That's also poppycock. You happen to know more about everything than anyone else ever has or ever will. There's no such thing as hard work or industriousness that allows a man or woman to acquire a skill. Artisanship? Skilled craftsmanship that can create beauty? Big freaking deal. You know that you could do it better if you only bothered to try, and if you don't try, then that's because it's not worth doing in the first place.

Gray hairs and calluses mean nothing to you. With your childlike youth (no matter your age), you can do better at anything than anyone else can or ever will. So scoff at age and experience. No one's got anything to teach you. You might hear that you shouldn't honk at an old geezer because maybe when he was young he risked his life for our country. Or maybe you shouldn't blow some old biddy off the sidewalk because she's devoted her whole life to caring for others. What's the difference? This world isn't about anyone else but you and what's easiest for you. If respect for others older than you are gets in your way, the heck with it. Plus, old people are often really weak and timid, and you can and should push them around just because you can.

Okay. Enough said. Just don't fall for that stupid trap of respecting age. What good will it do you? And, of course, you'll never get old yourself, so you don't need to worry about karma. You know what karma really is, anyway? It's whatever you want or need it to be for *you*.

29

Show Everyone
Around You That You're
Holier Than Thou

Don't hide the halo. When anyone in your path does something you don't like, cite some passages from the Bible that make it clear that the other person is evil or a fool. When you're criticized (imagine!), quote some prayer or line from Scripture that compares your martyrdom with that of a famous saint. When you're served a dish of some kind at your friends' home, bring up some moral objection to eating it. This accomplishes the dual function of making your hosts feel bad for having wasted their time, and also making them feel as if they're spiritually deficient. This double whammy guarantees that you'll be considered superior to everyone in your world. So what if they resent you for making them feel lowly? Don't the great prophets and saviors always end up being persecuted? Is that not by itself a clear sign of your elevated position?

If you're in a house of worship, pray louder than everyone else. If the prayer is in a foreign language, make sure you speak up really loudly so other people will know you're proficient in Latin or Hebrew or whatever. If some political issue arises in conversation, such as waging war on terrorists, stop the conversation cold by saying that you're too pious and holy to even think about wars where people get hurt or killed. If anyone near you is discussing the stock market and you don't feel for the moment like bragging about your investment prowess, simply say that you don't feel like talking about "sordid money matters."

And if some fool whom you borrowed money from asks for it back, perhaps you can look at him pityingly and say, "'Tis better to give than receive." And maybe add a few lines about how sorry you are that this person is such a money-obsessed Philistine. Then sigh and say you're really too busy thinking about the Bible to have to be concerned with repaying a few trivial earthly obligations right now. Then look heavenward and mention "usury."

This, by the way, is a simply great way to ruin a marriage. Just act as if, overnight, you've become morally superior to your spouse, and see how it makes him or her love you all the more.

The world needs to know that you're a holy being, above this earthly vale, and this might as well start at home. This especially applies to young people. You'll really make a big start toward the grandeur that's your due if you present yourself as being "above" your elders. Begin by simply saying that you won't eat your mother's cooking because she's murdered animals to make it. Watch her face fall and the color rise to her face. Then tell your father that, whatever he does, there's blood on his money. And remind all of the people in the neighborhood that they're killers and imperialists and you're better than they are, or simply imply it by your disdainful facial expressions.

Yes. You can *feel* the holiness surging through you, can't you? Enjoy it.

This works almost unimaginably well for people you've known for the better part of your life. Try waking up one morning as your husband is making you sausage and say to him, "I don't eat the flesh of living creatures, and neither would you if you had any decency."

Or, when your wife starts getting dressed to go out to work, ask her if she realizes that the lipstick she's wearing was tested on poor innocent rabbits who were tortured to death so that she could look nice! Or, if your next-door neighbors' son has just joined the military, tell them how nice it must be to have a child who's in training to kill innocent people overseas.

It sure does ring people's bells to be called names and to have you lord it over them with your self-important, holier-than-thou attitude. Try it for a while, and see how much the little people love and worship you, their new god or goddess. It should really bring a smile to your face.

❖ ❖ ❖

30

Fight the Good Fight
... Over Everything

Anything is worth fighting over. You have the blood of the Vikings or the Zulu or the Hebrew warriors or the Cherokee coursing through your veins. You're a killer. You're a man or woman who will brave anything to achieve the final victory. And no detail escapes your vision of triumph. That's why it's worth starting a fight over every little thing. Did the waiter bring the meat imperfectly broiled? Don't just send it back. Scream at him—and the maître d', too. Did your spouse get your shirts done with light starch instead of full starch? *This means war!* Berate the mate, and sue the cleaners—and the sooner the better. Did some jerk cut you off at the last light? Don't just mutter under your breath. Jump out of your car with a baseball bat and start swinging. Let a real brawl ensue.

Losers and wimps may try to tell you, "Hey, that's not worth fighting over." Well, maybe not for them—the good-for-nothin' weaklings! But you're strong and tough, and you always win. Plus, your majesty is of such grandeur that even the slightest affront to it is worth a fight. Many a geek and a nerd would say that if someone says 99 kind things about you but has one word of caution, you should ignore the latter. *No way!* You demand satisfaction. Out come the dueling pistols. Life and death hinge upon getting your way down to the last detail.

And please don't let long ties of blood or friendship stand in your way. If you've been insulted—no matter how trivially—you must fight over it, and fight to the death. Did your lover tell you she thinks of you "often during the day"? That's not good enough by a long shot. She should be thinking of you every second. Blast her for that! Did your boss tell you that you did a *pretty* good job on your assign-ment? What the hell does that mean? *"Pretty good"?* That ain't good enough. How dare he!

Always be on the highest alert for things to get your goat and irritate you, and you shall surely find them and fight the good fight. Stay in attack mode, and always be on the ready.

And don't count the cost, for heaven's sake. Do not, for example, ask yourself whether it's worth losing your job over a real or imagined slight. Just go ahead and spin out of control. So what if you lose your job? You'll get another. Is it worth losing your lover or a spouse's affections over an offhand remark? Of course it is. Nothing's going to get past you—no, sir.

Choose your battles? Heck, no. Why choose when you can fight *all* of them!

❖ ❖ ❖

31

Do It Your Way

You can do it in your special, unique way, no matter how anyone else does it. Just think of that old crooner, Frank Sinatra. He did it his way. So can you. There may be certain laughably obsolete, stolid, and boring conventions about the way you work your way up in a business or don't take on airs when you first join a company or move into a neighborhood. Ha! That's for other people. You just do it every and any old way that comes into your little head. You don't have to adjust to the rest of the world—the rest of the world has to adjust to *you*.

Is it really that complex? I mean, suppose you live out in Hollywood like yours truly. There's an audition for an acting role you really want, and you're called in. Well, don't get there on time. Arrive when you feel like it. And don't be respectful toward the people who are auditioning you. They're lucky you cared to show your face at a gathering of nobodies. And by all means, don't look neat and clean. Just wear some old, baggy warm-up clothes and let your stringy, oily hair hang down in your face. It wouldn't hurt if you walked in with a cigarette dangling from your mouth, too. That would be cool.

If you're in school and you want to do well in a class, don't pay any attention to what the teacher says. Don't even bother to read the homework assignments. Just do whatever you feel like doing and then get really huffy if your teacher cops an attitude about your work.

Looking for a mate? Treat any guy or doll who comes along like dirt. Just talk about yourself and never ask about them.

And on the job, laugh at your boss and make fun of her behind her back and also right in her face. Bosses like to be mocked by their employees. And anyway, who the heck cares what your boss thinks? Just do it your way, without regret or sorrow.

The whole world is watching to make sure you do it your way and no other. They never expected you to follow their routine. Humankind has been waiting for thousands of years for that one guy or doll who wouldn't knuckle under—and you're the Messiah of Doing Your Own Thing. All hail!

◈ ◈ ◈

32

Think the Worst of Everyone

Always expect the worst of everyone. Why not? You know that in their hearts, they're all rats and creeps who just can't wait to stick it to you. They're all snakes in the grass hoping against hope for a chance to do you in or sneak up behind your back and harm you in some way. Why give them the chance? Strike first by expecting that they'll do you wrong. Then you can easily justify being suspicious and sarcastic and nasty and untrusting. Plus, you can insult them and lie to them and make sure that you bring out the behavior that was just waiting for a chance to get out anyway.

Some fools say that if you expect the best from people, you'll often get it. What a silly, infantile lie. In fact, you should always assume that people have the worst possible motives, never tell the truth, and will act dishonestly if given half a chance. So, be smart about it. *Don't give them half a chance.* Be on guard, suspicious, and defensive right off the bat. Then they can't slip any tricks by you like pretending to be fairminded or generous or trustworthy. People sometimes do that for years on end, just to lull you into a false sense of security. Don't let it happen to you. Put a halt to any good behavior others might show you by erecting a wall between you and them, and then pour boiling oil on the invaders of your great kingdom, whoever they may be.

※ ※ ※

33

Live Above Your Means

Live it up. Now, this is probably simpler than you realize—it's even more basic than the rule about not saving any money. *You can afford anything you want just because you want it.* If you see it in a magazine, you deserve it. If you have a friend who has a car, then you deserve to have that automobile as well. If someone you know just went to Hawaii, you need to go there, too. The fact that you earn X entitles you to spend 150 percent of X. The fact that you have nothing in the bank (and why the heck should you?) cannot and *must not* stop you from buying anything you want. What are credit cards for? What's zero down payment for? It's for you, you, you to enjoy anything you want.

And please don't worry if you don't have the money to pay your bills. Just apply for a new credit card and transfer the balance to *that* card. Or borrow it from someone (but remember, don't pay it back), 'cause if you want to live in a certain lofty manner, there's no reason on earth why you shouldn't do so. Get hip to yourself. You deserve it all—and just because you have no clear way to pay for it, that's meaningless. Buy it anyway.

You are The Chosen One, and I guess I just have to keep telling you that, because you're so darned modest. The Chosen One will always be able to make money appear at the last moment, like the miracle of the loaves and the fishes. Miracles do happen where money is concerned. You can count on that. It's much more real than arithmetic or numbers on a credit card bill.

So go ahead. Live it up, and worry about tomorrow . . . tomorrow. Bottom line: Spend all you want—but don't save anything or you'll ruin the whole effect. It all adds up to a delicious sense of freedom.

34

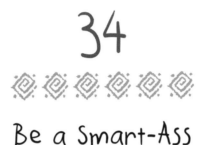

Be a Smart-Ass

You have to get in the last word, and the world needs your wisecracks. And don't let some sugary smooth talker keep you from doling out venom along with your wit. If some kindly fool utters a sweet comment to you, come right back at him with a smart-ass retort that will leave him gasping for breath. If he tells you your suit is nice, tell him he needs a new one. If he tells you your hair looks pretty, say, "I wish I could say the same for you," and then ask him when the last time was he saw a barber. If someone tells you she admires your car, tell her you hope she doesn't steal it. Add that if you had a car like hers, you'd be jealous, too.

While you're at it, make a joke out of everything. The world wants to hear you mock it from head to toe. If someone tells you that he's proud to be an American, remind him about slavery and ask him if he's proud of that, too. This performs the dual function of putting the guy in his place, showing how very clever you are, and also pointing out that you're holier than he could ever hope to be.

If a relative has put up some lovely religious statuary in her front yard, make some sarcastic remark about buying it at a thrift shop, and then ask in hushed tones if she realizes that she's being "anti" your religion by displaying it. This actually gets you a sort of hat trick: contempt, cutting off relationships, *and* showing what a wise guy you are.

There's a saying that the man who's a hero is the man who swallows a wisecrack. No. Not true. For everyone else, maybe, but not for you. The world needs to listen to your sneers and jeers—immediately and often. Other people should keep their traps shut—especially when they're around *you,* but you should feel completely comfortable humiliating and deriding everyone in your sphere.

※ ※ ※

35

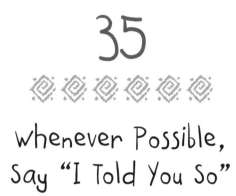

whenever Possible, Say "I Told You So"

Pour salt on those wounds. If something bad happens to someone you know, don't sympathize. Don't identify. Don't share the pain. Instead, simply say, "I told you so," and explain how you would never have been duped into whatever evil befell the other person. The world needs to know that whatever they did wrong—however innocently or unavoidably—*you* wouldn't have done it, and you know better. It might smart a bit for others to hear it, but they need to know that there is a superior being among them who doesn't make the kind of mistakes they do. It does them good to know this. People will respect you and fear you more if you make them feel really bad about who they are. And saying "I told you so" is the perfect way to accomplish that feat.

❖ ❖ ❖

(I bet you thought you couldn't ruin
your life in just 35 simple steps, right?
Well, I told you so. Just <u>kidding!</u>)

❖ ❖ ❖ ❖ ❖ ❖

AFTERWORD

Well, you're almost there. If you've been reading carefully, and if you've been thinking of ways to put all of these steps into action, you're well on your way to making the one and only life you have . . . ruinous. But there are just a few other little thoughts (and one big one) that make the scheme of self-destruction complete. First, in every situation, ask yourself, "Am I considering other people's welfare? Am I taking into account their points of view?" If you're doing either, you're probably not going to ruin your life quickly enough. You should also ask, "Am I acting like a big baby, or am I acting like a grown-up here?" If you're acting at all like an adult, you're also not doing yourself in well enough.

The key in every case is to be obsessed, selfish, and immature. When you find yourself acting with kindness, generosity, prudence, or common sense, you're probably way off base and might even be wandering into the rules for making your life a success. That would be a grave error.

Now, let's be fair. It's entirely possible that you might accidentally show some selflessness or care in some situations, but not if you're always on guard. You might actually be empathetic if you don't remember to get down into a good defensive posture of mistrust right away. So, be lazy and rude and a spendthrift all at once by doing something like using money you should be putting aside for education for drinks and drugs—thereby jeopardizing your future, the lives of those around you, and society as a whole.

Finally, and most important: Don't believe in God. Or, to put it more precisely, believe and know in your heart that there *is* a God—and you are the One. This is really key to every other part of this little guidebook. Believe that you are the most important One, that everything you do is what counts, that no traditions or laws man-made or natural apply to you, and that neither mathematics nor the laws of physics nor medicine apply to you. And sure as shootin', you'll find yourself ruined. Believe that you control all of human destiny. Believe that you can determine the results of everything that happens on this earth. Believe that the whole world is one giant movie and you're the director. And, know that you're the boss, the puppet master, controlling every single aspect of everyone's life: chief critic, dictator, censor, and of course, beneficiary and inheritor of everyone else's labor. You're a pagan god of sorts, with no responsibility to anyone in return. You're not the god of love or compassion. You're the god who lolls about eating grapes someone else has peeled, deriving your pleasure from everyone else's sacrifice and owing nothing in return.

Then, and only then, will you truly understand who you are. And then—God help you.

※ ※ ※ ※ ※ ※

How to Ruin Your Love Life

[**Author's Note:** I've alternated the use of male and female pronouns throughout the book to avoid the awkwardness of the "he/she" construction, and also to avoid disparaging one gender over the other. Be assured, however, that all of these essays apply to both sexes.]

1

Know That Your Wishes Are the Only Ones That Matter in Any Situation

Something that you're going to have to get into your little pumpkin head is that your lover basically exists to help you. He has no meaningful life independent of what he can do for you. Yes, your lover may have what some might see as personal interests, hobbies, needs, wishes, and fears, but those aren't important. What *is* important, what *does* count, is what your lover can *do for you*. If he's interested in playing tennis or buying antiques or watching the Tampa Bay Buccaneers on TV, that's worthy of some tiny, passing notice. And if he has some desire to live a life that has some modicum of independence to it, that's also interesting, ho-hum. You might acknowledge it with a cursory nod and a wave.

But what really counts in any relationship is *you!* What *you* want from the relationship is what matters. What *you* want out of your lover is what always comes first in any and every situation.

If your lover wants to stay home and listen to opera—or even sing along with Ludacris on the stereo—that's nice, and you might say how cute he is for having that desire. But what really matters is what *you* want to do. If you decide that you simply have to go shopping for furniture on this particular day, then that's what you're both going to do. If you have to go to the mall and want to drag your lover along, no matter how unhappy he looks, then that's the deciding vote. (By the way, you *always* cast the deciding vote about everything.) If you want to go to a friend's house and watch old movies and drink cocktails on a Saturday night while your lover sits home alone, then that's the way it has to be.

If you feel that you don't want to go on a vacation and your lover does, then just stay home and watch him stew in his own juices. You see, your goal here is to express in words and actions that *your* wishes are the only ones that matter.

The truth is that your "love object" is incredibly, unbelievably lucky to have you in his life. Just for this unworthy soul to be associated with you is such a grand honor that you don't really need to pay any further attention to his desires.

Plus, the truth is, and this is so important
that it deserves its own rule . . .

2

Rest Assured That You Know Better about Every Subject Than Your Lover

This is not particularly a matter of education or who went to what college or graduate school. This is not about your thinking that you know better because you have a Ph.D. in psychology and your lover is a high-school dropout. No, this has to do with the fact that you, just for being *you*, know better than your lover about everything. You know better about sports, food, and clothing. You know better about her family. You especially know better about her friends.

You just plain know better about everything. You can save a lot of future aggravation and pain if you just make that clear early on. Yes, you may listen briefly to your lover's opinions (never facts—always, at best, opinions) and nod politely and pityingly at them. But are they truly deserving of being heard? Is it really worth the time of someone as smart as you to hear such low-order blathering? I don't think so, and neither do you.

You know better about who to hang out with, who to be around, who not to be around, where to live, what to buy, and what not to buy.

And you know what? Get that idea out in the open right away. Don't waste a moment with any kind of fake solicitude for your lover's nattering. Just express here and now that you're the smart one in the relationship and things will go better for both of you.

You see, the sad truth is that if your lover gets the idea into her head that her ideas are worth anything, then she's going to be as disappointed as can be when you finally have to bring the hammer down and let her know that, in fact, her ideas are, well, not quite "worthless," but not really up to your level or anything close to it. If you can get her acclimated right away to the crucial truth that she really has very little of worth to say on anything important, then you're far ahead of the game in terms of time-saving and getting lines of authority set down neatly.

> *And please don't be worried about hurting her feelings because, if I may make so obvious a point, you can . . .*

3

Live Your Life As If Only <u>Your</u> Feelings Count!

Now, I don't for a moment mean to say that your lover doesn't have any feelings. That would be totally incorrect and an insult to the whole idea of humanity. All human beings have feelings. In fact, the key to what distinguishes human beings from rocks and stones is that humans have feelings. Your lover *does* have feelings of joy, exhilaration, fear, loss, torment, and despair. Have no doubt about that. The only thing is that those feelings don't really count for much in the grand scheme of things. Oh, sure, to him, those feelings may seem important at the moment, but overall, in the big picture, your lover's feelings just don't mean very much. After all, *you* are not feeling them!

No, *you* are feeling *your* feelings, and those are the ones that matter. In fact, each feeling you have counts for about 1,000 times as much as each feeling that your lover has. Again, this is simply because *you* can feel *your* own feelings and you cannot—if you are in the mood to ruin your love life at all—feel his.

Now, those are some of the Grand Rules of Disengagement, the overarching principles that govern how your relationship with your lover will be run so that it cannot possibly last. But there are dozens of smaller rules governing specific situations, and you need to hear about these to really wreck your love life.

Let's try a few of them. . . .

4

Point Out Your Lover's Imperfections in Public

You've probably been very restrained about pointing out your lover's failings up till now. You've no doubt observed them, catalogued them, and made them into neat lists in your head. But most likely, out of some excess of politeness, you've refrained from revealing each one to her. Maybe you didn't want to start an argument when other people weren't around, because what would be the point? You want *others* to notice how totally right you are, too. An audience of one just doesn't cut it. After all, what's the point of noting that your girlfriend never dresses in coordinated clothes and has a blubber roll if there's no one there to cheer you on and laugh appreciatively at your verbal repartee and biting wit? Entertainers act in front of cheering throngs, not in closets.

That's why it's urgent that you save up all of your gripes and unload them all at once on your lover when other people are nearby. For example, suppose you think that your girlfriend is a little too close to her mother and talks to her on the phone far too much. Fine. The best time to make that observation is not when the two of you are alone together. No, how can you get a laugh out of a grown woman you've just accused of being a big baby? You can't. Wait until you have friends over for dinner. Wait until you're at a cocktail party slurping down Grey Goose. Then, when everyone's a bit tipsy and in a mood to laugh, say, "Oh, Cindy wouldn't even dream of going through a day without talking to her mother. She wrote the book on being Mother's perfect little girl. Not that I mind, but she *is* 38, so you might think she could go through a day without asking her mommy what to wear every day."

That way, you get a few laughs. Plus, you brand your lover as a weak, immature, ineffectual female whose friends all now know it to be true. How *clever* you are!

Now she's probably going to be a little ticked off at you when you get home that night. After all, you've just humiliated her in front of her friends. She might even berate you for it.

Well, that's when you get to lay in your next ultra-cool step to ruining your love life and make it happen in living color. . . .

5

Never Admit That You're Wrong or Apologize in Any Dispute

Why should you ever admit that you're wrong? You are *never* wrong. Just the fact that *you* did it or said it or forgot to do it makes it right. That, by itself, converts wrong to right. Maybe you recall your high school teachers teaching you about "the divine right of kings," which basically meant that they were appointed by God and could do no wrong. Well, that was long abolished by revolutions, and heads rolled that were supposedly divinely blessed. But *you* still have that divine right, and it means that you're never, ever wrong.

Now, let's imagine that your boyfriend starts in on you by accusing you of humiliating him in front of his friends at a public gathering. Well, just laugh at him some more, and tell him he's a wimp for not being able to take a joke. Or tell him that when you called him a mama's boy in front of his college buddies and he didn't get a kick out of it, well, that just proves how weak and overly sensitive he is.

Or, let's say the shoe's on the other foot. Suppose you're the guy and you've just said—in front of your friends—that your girlfriend or wife is a total slob who can't even keep her shoe rack straight, let alone balance a checkbook. And it just so happens that she works as a bookkeeper at a shoe store, so the criticism, leveled in front of her colleagues from The Shoe Giant really stings. And she tells you so. What do you do? Well, you simply say, "Hey, if the shoe fits, wear it." Or else, just look at her sternly and say, "I guess you just can't take the truth, right? I'm just trying to help, but if you can't accept the fact that you're a slob, then I guess that just shows how insecure you are. Maybe that's the source of your slobbiness."

(By the way, human beings love to be told how insecure they are. It makes them feel swell. Try it over and over again—you'll be amazed by how it makes people love you.)

Or else just say, "Hey, I call 'em like I see 'em, and if you can't take it, tough."

The main idea is that you should absolutely refuse to apologize for being wrong . . . because you never are. The burden is always on your lover to simply take your criticism and bear it.

And if you won't admit that her feelings have any merit, that's just fine. Your lover should get used to the idea that what she has to say means zilch, nothing, and that any expectation that you'll pay real attention to what she says is a joke.

Just forget apologies no matter what you do, and this doesn't just apply to what you say. Suppose you come home drunk and knock over your wife's favorite vase and smash it. Don't apologize. If you crash into your husband's car in the garage, for goodness' sake, don't say you're sorry.

If your wife catches you flirting with her co-worker, don't apologize. You owe it to yourself to never admit you're wrong. It might give you some kind of complex if you start doing so. Just don't do it, period. If you said it or did it, or didn't say it or didn't do it, that makes it right.

6

Overdramatize Everything

Turn everything that happens to you into high drama. Don't let anything just be a normal part of someone's day. No, you have to have excitement and turbulence in your life. If your lover does the slightest thing you don't like, make it into a huge scene filled with anguish and recrimination. If she does anything that's even slightly wrong around the house, make it into an aggravated crime. There's nothing that you can't make into the mad scene of Ophelia in *Hamlet* if you really try. Make your mate really suffer and sweat bullets over any little thing that goes amiss in your life. It's not just an incident—it's the stuff of horror movies, and don't you forget it.

Be sure to save up all of your energy for these scenes. If your lover overfills a cup of tea, scream as if she's just pulled a gun on you. If she asks you about something you charged on your joint credit card, have a fit and scream at the top of your lungs that what you do is none of her business. If she asks if you want to see a movie, act as if she's insulted you by suggesting that you go see that piece of cinematic trash.

It's also important to make a huge deal about everything that happened to you during the day when you come home from work. Turn every event into the shower scene from *Psycho* so that it's really unpleasant and tense for your lover to have a conversation with you. This makes total sense. It allows you to occupy the stage and to give yourself the lead role in whatever drama you've decided to play out that day. You don't need to audition or go to acting school. You can have your drama anytime you want—and if it's too much for your lover to bear on a constant basis, too bad. If you want to go into hysterics recalling the conversation you had with your boss that day, go for it.

You have the right to create unpleasant, irrational dramas in your life any and all of the time. That is your right as a diva, male or female.

7

♡♡♡♡

Demand Expensive Gifts from Your Lover

That's right. Just having your boyfriend love you, praise you, or pay attention to you isn't enough. You want something tangible that you can actually put in your jewelry box or on your stereo shelf. Don't let him get away with just saying or doing sweet things. No, you want the equivalent of gold doubloons that the pirate captain would bite on to make sure it was real gold. You want something that you can show off to your friends—and how can you wear a sweet phrase around your neck?

There's a great song about diamonds being a girl's best friend—and you know what? It's totally true. Diamonds *are* a girl's best friend. But gold rings and fancy cars and pearl necklaces are nice, too.

Now suppose your boyfriend can't afford to give you lavish presents. Well, then mock and belittle him—preferably in front of other people. Now you're getting it. Nothing should inhibit you from letting fly with some really caustic comments if you're not getting the goods. How's this for a good one: "My last boyfriend always gave me gold jewelry, but Tom here has never even taken me out to a five-star restaurant for dinner!"

In today's world, talk is cheap. But money walks the walk *and* talks the talk. That's why you need some concrete evidence of how much your lover cares for you in the form of something with a fancy price tag. Only if you can gaze at something really extravagant on your wrist or in your study can you be sure that you're getting all you truly deserve.

8

Never Be Grateful for the Gifts You <u>Do</u> Get

True, they may have been a major drain on his salary. Yes, they may have required her to work overtime to pay for the gifts. But if you act really grateful, that implies some sense of duty or obligation on your part. Bad idea! Just accept the gifts you receive, give correct but not effusive thanks, and let it be known that you expect even better next time.

That way, you let your lover know that he's never quite adequate, never quite getting all the way there in terms of making you happy—and that he has to try harder next time.

Now, some may say, "Hey, isn't love about *sharing?* Isn't it about taking up burdens and bearing them jointly? It's not about just one of you exploiting the other, is it?"

> *Well, I'm so glad you brought that up.*
> *Because the truth is . . .*

9

Carve It in Stone: Love Relationships Aren't Partnerships— They're Master-Servant Relationships, and You Are the Master (or Mistress)

What kind of fun is it if you have to share things? How is it fair to be expected to do as much for the other person as he does for you?

I mean, how do you come out ahead in that situation?

No, you're owed everything you can get from the relationship, and in return, you're supposed to give as little as humanly possible and still generate enough interest to get the gifts and the attention and adoration. Imagine the relationship between a master and a slave in the old South—and there you have your template of the kind of relationship you should have. You get the adoration, and he gets the opportunity to adore. You get the gifts, and he gets the opportunity to *give* the gifts. It makes a lot of sense, don't you think?

You know, the world is an amazingly complex place. You can't figure it out in any meaningful sense. The only thing you have to pay attention to in your relationships—which can be richly complex, too—is *what's in it for you*. If you can always look at every situation in terms of what *you* can get out of it, *you* will be far, far ahead of the game.

Don't look at the relationship in terms of what you can do for your significant other. In fact, don't even think about the other as "significant" at all. What counts is what you get for yourself *out* of the other, and that keeps things at a simple, manageable level. If you were to express wild gratitude for what you got in the way of gifts or services, that would screw up everything. If you think of your relationship as a partnership where you owe as much as you get, that makes you tired just thinking about it.

Love isn't a partnership; it's an owner/owned situation . . . and you are definitely the owner.

10

Compare Your Lover with Lovers You've Dated in the Past

Be sure to negatively compare your current lover with those you've had in the past in terms of lovemaking ability, generosity, power, looks, and connections. Don't compliment your current mate in any way. Instead, specifically point out what you miss about your last lover—how she looked like a *Penthouse* centerfold, how she stayed in bed with you for hours giving you more pleasure than you could have ever dreamed of—and wistfully recall just how indescribably delicious it all was. Just make sure your current girlfriend really knows how deficient she is based on the high standards that were set by those before her.

Now, you can really make this pay off big in terms of wrecking your love life if you combine two rules: Talk about how bad your current lover is, and do so in front of your friends. For instance, a good line is, "Suzy is such a killjoy. My old girlfriend, Delilah, liked to get really drunk, take off her blouse, and dance on the bar in her bra in front of the whole restaurant . . . but Suzy's a big dud."

It really doesn't matter *what* you say that compares your old lover with your new one. The whole point is that you want your lover to know in her heart that you're always secretly comparing her with someone else—and consistently finding something lacking. That inspires fear, resentment, loathing, and confusion, virtually guaranteeing an explosion of some sort, or at least severe depression somewhere down the pike. But do it anyway! Constantly keep your new gal in the insecure and hopeless maze of trying to live up to someone from your past.

And if she challenges you with, "Well, if your last girlfriend was so darned great, why aren't you with her now?" then just answer with raised eyebrows, or perhaps a slightly wistful look that implies, "Oh, how I wish I were!" That should set your lover back one or two paces, tee-hee.

11

Talk about Yourself Exclusively

Suppose your lover calls you up in the middle of the workday to ask how you're feeling or just to share the communion of two loving souls. Well, don't buy it! You need to make it clear right from the start that the call is an excuse for you to talk ad nauseam about your latest problems with your co-worker or your boss or the woman who sells you bagels in the morning. Your points of view, what you have to complain about, what you have to brag about—that's all that matters. Don't let yourself get sucked into the silly idea that there should be any equality in the conversation or that you should actually show any real interest in your lover's issues. No, that would be insane.

Let's face it: It's really boring to listen to other people's problems. But for other people to hear *your* problems, now that's truly fascinating. Why is there a difference? Because *your* problems are about *you*, and that makes them far more interesting than what anybody else has to say.

Now, you may have heard that good listeners make good lovers. Or that good lovers are good listeners. Don't you believe it. Your lover's function is to be a good listener. *Your* function is to talk. And don't even slow down to hear a word about what's going on with him. Just let fly with all of your issues and concerns, and if he finds himself unable to listen any longer, just sulk in silence.

And by the way, you don't have to be original in your analysis of your problems. Feel totally free to repeat the same old stories and the same old grievances day after day, hour after hour. If your lover truly cares for you, those tales should be just as new and exciting to him the hundredth time as the first. Just talk and talk and talk, and then when you get bored, say you have to get off the phone.

This is your right. And if your lover says that it's urgent that you listen to him talk about some crisis of his, all you have to do is listen for a few seconds, then interrupt with, "Hey, that reminds me of what my sister did today. Can you believe her?!" And then launch into a diatribe of what your sister did to make you crazy.

Let your lover just stuff his feelings. It will do him good to realize that listening to you will enrich his life far more than talking ever could.

12

Remember That Your Lover Is Your Punching Bag

We all have issues and crises that come up in the course of a day. That's normal, and it's just the way the world works. After all, it's frustrating and difficult to be a human being. We get dressed down by our bosses. We encounter bad drivers on the freeway. We often don't feel very well. We worry about money and mortality and weight. This is the natural course of life. And, just as naturally, this mortal life builds up anger and crises of the emotions and spirit. All of this means that we have to vent that anger and frustration somehow.

But how? We can't yell at our boss or we might get fired. We can't yell at our co-workers or we might get the reputation (however false!) of being difficult to get along with. That might inhibit promotions or pay increases or might get us demoted. We can't just go out on the street and start screaming. This might get us locked up or shot (if we live in a place where unusual behavior leads to police shootings). We can't just start throwing our trash out on the street, even if it does mimic what we feel in our hearts.

So what do we do? Simple! We take it out on our lover! I mean, what was she put on the planet for except to be a punching bag, a bayonet practice dummy for our disappointments, worries, and fears? Yes! Get it in your head! Your lover exists to be screamed at and emotionally battered.

Suppose your boss reprimands you for screwing up a contract. Fair enough. This can happen at any time in the busy corporate world. Your task, after that happens, is to grin and bear it for the rest of the day, and then, when you get home, really let your mate have it. Take her to task over a messy kitchen or a leaky faucet or a joke that you didn't find funny, and just let it all out in any way you see fit. Remember, your lover is there to absorb your frustration with life like a sponge. If you know this and truly act on it, you'll feel a lot better. And who cares what kind of day she had? She's there for *you*, not the other way around. So when those bad days come around—and they will for all of us, due to health or finances or work or worry about the mortal condition—just bury it inside for a good long time, and then, whaaam, let it fly.

And if she threatens to call the police, be sure to whine and apologize and promise never to do it again—until the next time.

13

Act Moody and Sulky when Your Lover Gets Home— but Don't Tell Him Why You're Sulking!

Yes, that's it—keep him guessing! Make him play 20 questions! Keep him in a state of agony. Give monosyllabic answers or none at all when he asks you what's wrong. Just walk from room to room slamming doors. Be certain he knows nothing about why you're feeling the way you are. In fact, why not just sulk and be uncommunicative even if you're feeling fine. The idea is to keep your lover constantly off balance and make him wonder what's going on and what he did wrong. That way, you can keep him under your thumb even more than usual.

Look at it this way: It's your lover's job to guess what's on your mind, to be constantly appealing to you for clemency, to be humbled by your power. Part of that power consists of mystification, puzzlement, and bewilderment on his part. Use that power to keep him humbled. Act like a magician, and constantly hide what's going on beneath your hat so that your lover feels lost and confused all of the time, wondering what he might have done wrong to make you so unhappy.

Make sure he knows that it's his duty to be constantly on bended knee before your moods and contrariness, and that life will just continue like this forever. It's not as if you owe him any explanations—he should be able to read your mind and know exactly what's wrong with you!

14

Remember That Your Lover Is Also Your Assistant, Lawyer, Placement Officer, Apartment Finder, and Loan Broker

Your lover isn't just there to help you with the little problems of life or to hold you tight on lonely nights. No, you see, your lover really *works for you!*

She may have another job at some office or store or factory, true. But that's just a sideline. Her main job in life is to make your life easier.

For example, if she has a family friend or an "in" at a certain firm that she was counting on to help her get a new job, don't let her be selfish about it. That connection exists for *your* benefit, not hers! Or what if you need a new space to live and affordable apartments are hard to find? Well, then your lover simply has to spring into action. It's her duty to call all of her friends to help you find a place to live. And have her stay up all night doing it! Don't let her beg off because she's tired or sick—that's a sign of weakness, and it won't be tolerated. Remember, your lover works for *you,* and that means *all* the time, not just when she feels up to it. And, yes, the job includes lending you money without getting repaid.

She also needs to be right there providing you with legal and financial advice when required, and it's her duty to function as your personal assistant: That is, it's her responsibility to make your doctor and dentist appointments, to book your plane and restaurant reservations—basically anything you need done—and God forbid if she forgets to do something or flubs the job. Really let her have it. So what if you don't pay her for her services? She should be *happy* to work for you without pay. It's a privilege to make your life run smoothly!

This connects closely with the next crucial step in ruining your love life. . . .

15

Don't for a Moment Let Your Lover Believe That He's Valued Just for Himself

Never let your lover think that for a minute. Far from it.

No! No! No! Never allow the slightest bit of complacency to enter his heart: He's valued for what he can do for *you*—and don't let him forget it! It's not about his fine character and how much he cares about you—it's about what he does for you in

147

concrete, preferably economic, terms.

And certainly don't let your lover act as if he can get away with just being a great guy or gal without actually doing something *big* for you. For example, suppose your lover is one of the most decent, upstanding men in the community. Let's imagine that he owns a small factory and one of his employees does something really stupid at work. That employee brings his mobile home into the factory, then starts to do some welding work on the home. He works so carelessly that he starts a fire that destroys a good chunk of the plant. But your lover is such a great guy that he not only doesn't press charges or fire the worker, but he actually takes the fire-starting employee into his home and gives him a place to live—and even puts him in charge of rebuilding the factory!

Yeah? *So what good did that do for you?* So what if your lovers's a saint with other people? What has he done for *you* lately? What has he done that helps you get a new job or a new car or diamond jewelry?

Don't let him rest on his laurels and feel like a hero. Let him know that he has to do something concrete for you so his day will be complete. And you don't want to hear these nauseating feel-good stories about other people anyway. What a bunch of sappy treacle!

Here's another one: Let's say your lover has an elderly, somewhat confused father who's walking down the street at nighttime in dark clothes—on a rural road no less. A driver speeds around the corner, hits him, puts him in the hospital, and he dies a few days later. Your lover could raise hell and sue. Instead, he goes to the unlucky driver and tells her that the accident wasn't her fault. Then he totally forgives her and wishes her well. As a result, the entire community praises him for his forbearance.

Don't let these actions fool you for a minute. What on earth does all of this Good Samaritan behavior do for *you?*

Let your lover know the truth: He can't get away with these pitifully saintly acts when he's supposed to be taking care of you night and day! That, and that alone, is his job, and if he doesn't do it well enough, let him know it in no uncertain terms.

16

Play Phone Games—
That Is, Don't Return Her
Calls So She Can See How
Cool and Aloof You Are

There used to be a saying that went something like this: "No one was ever killed over the telephone." (It was said to me by a friend in high school.) But how wrong that is! You can wound and maim and torture and hound and hurt and maybe even kill as a result of your shenanigans over the phone. You can do the obvious: not return calls and make your lover crazy. You can make her beg and plead to have you return the call. You can be even more clever: You can make her absolutely insane by letting her make several phone calls, while you make one call at some odd time that keeps her from possibly responding to it—and then have her make ten more calls that you don't answer at all.

Now, I, your humble servant, know very well that you might be saying to yourself, "Hey, that sounds like junior high school stuff. Aren't we supposed to be more mature than that?" No! *Love is a junior high school game!* If you acknowledge that right now, then you know a lot more than most people—and you certainly know more about how to ruin your love life than your lover or any of your "friends."

Another phone game you can play is a lot of fun: When your lover has just about had it and is about to jump off a bridge, you can just nonchalantly call as if nothing's happened, and if she asks where the heck you've been, just say, "Oh, I've been busy at work," and don't say any more about it! Tee-hee!

The phone-game rule is really a lot more cunning than it sounds, because it epitomizes the essence of a screwed-up love relationship: taking a potentially adult, mature union to the level of a seventh-grade competition to see who can get the better of the other. Try it, and you'll be amazed at how well it works.

Maybe human beings can't be killed over the telephone, as my childhood friend Marvin reminded me 44 years ago—but relationships surely can be.

17

Make Fun of Your Lover's Family

To you, maybe, your family is sacrosanct. Your parents are the ones who gave you birth and sustained you, and despite your occasional anger and frustration with them, you love them a lot. You would certainly not take kindly to anyone mocking them. This is all very well and good and totally understandable. But the fact that your family is precious to you doesn't mean a thing when it comes to belittling the members of your *lover's* family.

Have they failed to show you due deference and respect in every situation? Have they neglected to behave as if you were a god? Have they ever put any other interest ahead of you? Have they ever been less than prompt about serving you your meals when you came over to their house? Have they ever talked about themselves before they inquired about you? If so, then don't spare the sarcasm and cruelty.

Off with their heads! Show them no mercy whatsoever. They've behaved abominably, and don't hesitate to let your lover know it.

Did his parents fail to get you the gift you wanted for your birthday or Christmas or Hanukkah or Kwanzaa? Then they surely deserve to have you skewer them unmercifully every time their names are brought up. Or put it like this: Have they ever failed to acknowledge that their son is unbelievably, phenomenally lucky to have you in his miserable life? Then they deserve to be criticized unmercifully.

In fact, why wait for a special occasion? Why not just make cruel fun of them anytime it comes into your head to say anything at all? Why not make it a staple of your dialogue with your lover to mock and belittle his family—especially his mother and father—whenever you can squeeze it in?

Now, your lover may wince and protest. But that just shows that it's time to invoke an earlier rule and start belittling him for being a mama's boy. That's right—make him feel even worse than he already does!

Don't hold back when it comes to discussion of brothers or sisters either. It's true that some people feel an unbreakable bond with their siblings, and this may, in fact, apply to you. Perhaps your big brother rescued you from some mean kids on the playground when you were a tyke, or your sister once gave you $100 so you could buy a new outfit for the school dance. Whatever the case, you might very well feel extremely attached to your kin. And that's just fine.

But when it comes to your lover's siblings, that's a whole different kettle of fish. Those brothers or sisters exist solely for your belittlement. Mock their accents. Show contempt for their achievements or lack of them. Point out their failings, and here it doesn't matter if the failings are real or imagined. Just make a case for whatever's wrong with them, and you can be certain that your lover will just bow his head and take it. I've said it before and I'll say it again: Do not treat your lover the way you want to be treated (excuse me, *demand* to be treated!). For heaven's sake, treat him like the doormat he is. (After all, what other kind of human being would have you, but let's keep that little secret to ourselves!)

So, feel no compunction whatsoever about treating your lover's family to a daily roasting—in front of your lover and whoever else is available to listen.

Good, that's settled.

18

Let It Be Known That You Consider Affection to Be a Chore

Yes, this one's a killer! Make sure that your lover knows very well that you would rather do almost anything else than hug her, kiss her, or make love to her.

Of course, if you feel like it, you'll *do it.* At least, occasionally. But that doesn't mean you have to *like* doing it.

"All right, all right," you'll say with a sigh, "I guess we can make love, but we'll have to make it fast because I have an early meeting in the morning."

Or, try this: "Really? But didn't we just do it a week or two ago?" Or "Aww, I sort of felt like having a drink and watching *Jimmy Kimmel Live* instead. But if you insist, let's get it over with." Or "Well, all right. But I do have this rash. . . ."

Let your lover know beyond any shadow of a doubt that affection isn't something you crave because you're having loving feelings or just want to feel the closeness that having sex with your mate brings. Instead, act as if affection is just a gift that you'll grant—on special occasions—to your lover out of a sense of *noblesse oblige* and not out of any need for intimacy.

This one is a perfect, shimmering gem. It keeps your lover off balance—as so many of these suggestions do—and makes certain that she knows that she's on a short leash, is way near the end of that leash, and you can jerk it back to catch her up in a noose of low self-esteem at any time.

Affection—that is, physical affection—is basic to relationships in most cases. To make sure your lover knows you grant it only grudgingly and at your own sweet discretion is an ideal way to keep the relationship on consistently uncertain and uneasy terms.

So starting right now, keep her writhing in confusion and doubt so that you'll truly have the upper hand!

Now, this one is so important that I think I might even italicize it. Yes, I think I will, actually:

19

If You're Dating Someone Who Has a Lot of Problems, Is Generally a Mess, and All of Your Friends Dislike Him, Get Married Anyway— Marriage Will Cure All of Your Problems!

Now it may be true that you've heard just the opposite—that is, that marrying someone with a lot of problems is a recipe for disaster because his problems will only continue and probably even get worse in the hothouse atmosphere of marriage. You may have heard that people don't change once they get married, and you'll just be locked in legally to someone with a lot of baggage.

Nonsense! The moment the minister, priest, rabbi, or justice of the peace says, "I now pronounce you husband and wife," all of your lover's flaws and problems will vanish like the mist off Malibu Beach after lunch. You won't have any more problems with his lying or drinking. No. You'll never again have to deal with his laziness and refusal to get a job. And you won't have to worry about his propensity for reckless spending, gambling, cheating, and occasional stealing (from your wallet). Absolutely not. From the moment you say "I do," your mate will suddenly become a perfect, divine being with stellar character.

And how does this miracle occur, you might ask? *Because, you see, marriage changes people so completely that they become model citizens in an instant.*

Now, it's conceivable that even *you* have some flaws, or at least some doubts about yourself and your abilities to be a good marriage partner. It doesn't matter—get married anyway!

All of your problems and self-doubt will vanish into nothingness if you believe in the marriage fairy. Count on the magical powers inherent in reciting those marriage vows (and having a really expensive wedding that puts your parents into debt for years) and you'll be *saved* (no evangelist needed)!

Just remember: Whatever your issues, whatever your mate's issues, marry anyway! That's a sure way to wreck your love life, so go ahead and do it now.

20

Don't Ever Tell Your Lover, "I Love You"

Why should you utter those three insignificant words? Don't you have any short-term memory? I just told you a few pages back that love was a junior high school game. Why didn't you believe me?

What that meant was that although your lover is expected to constantly tell *you* that she loves you, you never have to reply in kind. Make her pant for it. Make her beg (similar to stingily doling out affection)! Make her yearn desperately for even a hint of "I love you." Yes, it's true that it gives you a certain amount of satisfaction to hear your lover say she adores you. There's something rather pleasurable about getting e-mails at work that close with a loving sentiment. But that doesn't mean you have to do anything in return, any more than you have to return phone calls promptly.

Repeat after me: Love is a junior high school game if you really want to do it well (and cruelly). So spare those three little words . . . and spoil the relationship.

21

Have a Relationship with Someone Who's Never Happy and Is Always Down in the Dumps . . . and Believe You Can and Will Make Him Happy

Yes, you may have heard that someone who's really down, gloomy, and angry all the time is doomed to stay that way. But that's not necessarily true in your case. *You* can change your lover simply by being in a relationship with him.

Now, this bit of advice is a little different from some of the previous rules. Usually, I tell you how to jam the other person's gears and make yourself the master. But in just this one case, let's reverse things a bit.

You see, in this situation, your lover is making you miserable on a consistent basis by engaging in many of the steps I've delineated up to this point. He's berating you, cheating on you, lying, being disrespectful, and disparaging your friends and family. Now a reasonable person might have seen this coming on when consistently faced with a grumpy, mean-spirited individual. But no, not *you!* You're convinced that you *will* change him and make him into a happy, chirpy little angel of light. You can be sure of it. Yes, maybe no one else can do it, but you can! You can actually change human personality just by being in his presence, and make him happy although there's no evidence that he's ever felt that emotion a day in his life.

Don't be swayed by naysayers, though. No, Pollyanna, just dedicate yourself to doing everything you can for your lover—although you're miserable all the while—and I promise that you'll be a happy, happy camper for the rest of your days.

(Yeah, right.)

Now, back to driving your lover crazy instead of driving yourself crazy . . .

22

Expect Your Lover to Look like Someone Out of a <u>Penthouse</u> Centerfold

Don't for a minute let your lover off the hook when it comes to appearance. That's right. *You* can gain as much weight as you want and sport long, shaggy, goofy-looking hair. But make sure she knows that you expect her to look fabulous at all times. She has to diet, work out, have plastic surgery, dye her hair—basically do anything and everything to keep up the facade. And you don't have to do anything but sit back and criticize!

That's your prerogative. Just be certain to really stay on top of the situation. Maybe tack up sample diets and exercise programs on the refrigerator door, or give her articles to read that you find in magazines such as *Shape* and *Self* about makeovers and liposuction. And don't forget to tack centerfolds from *Playboy* or *Penthouse* in the den or bathroom to show her just how inadequate she is. Also be sure to bring up the subject of friends or acquaintances who used to be ". . . you know, obese, like you . . ." and got themselves straightened out by some superhuman feat of self-discipline—or maybe by having their intestines stapled.

You can be confident that your lover will be happy to be frequently told how she can perfect her appearance. People like to be reminded of their flaws—especially by their lovers. And don't forget to pinch her upper arm or her thigh every once in a while to remind her that she's got extra fat in those areas—everyone loves that!

By letting your lover know that you think she could be perfected in some very basic ways, she'll realize how incredibly lucky she is that you tolerate her. She'll feel permanently ill at ease, knowing that on any given day you might dump her for someone who's better looking. People really like that feeling of insecurity and of not being loved for themselves.

And one last thing to remember: Your lover, as noted previously, is a punching bag for you, so if you happen to feel some insecurity about your own appearance, why not take it out on her? (After all, this could inspire her to have plastic surgery on her nose, which she could really use!)

That makes sense, doesn't it? Make *her* feel bad all the time so you don't have to. You'll both be a lot happier.

23

♡♡♡♡

Feel Free to Say Any Cruel Thing You Want to Your Lover, and when Reproached about It, Say, "Hey, Can't I Even Express My <u>Feelings</u>?"

Yes, actually say *"feelings"* in a reverential way so that your lover knows that once the word is invoked, you can say anything you want and get away with it. When you're in the midst of voicing these all-important thoughts, nothing else can possibly be allowed to come in the way of that expression. Saying how you feel is as basic as breathing in and out, right? If your lover doesn't allow you to express those feelings, isn't he suffocating you? Of course he is!

So say anything you like—no matter how hurtful—and when your lover says, "That's a bit rude, isn't it?" respond with an outraged look and a haughty reply, such as: "Oh, I guess I'm not allowed to say anything at all, right? From now on, I'll just talk to my cat. She lets me say anything I want and doesn't jump down my throat."

Or else, say something really cutting, maybe about his mother or father, and then when he looks shocked, say, "I'm just trying to have a healthy relationship by expressing my feelings. But I guess that's not allowed. What am I supposed to do—keep it all bottled up inside me forever?! I don't think that would be healthy for either of us, do *you*?"

The beauty of this is that your lover really can't provide an adequate response to your "logic."

What's he going to say—"No, you're not *allowed* to express your feelings"? Of course not.

So, feel free to say or even do anything you want, and know you can get away with it. Why? Well, shucks, you're just expressing your feelings.

24

Forbid Your Lover to See Her Friends

Now, you may have heard some balderdash to the effect that friends are even more important than family, that friends are the family members we choose for ourselves. And, yes, maybe that's true. Some people can be extremely attached to their friends. I would imagine that you, dear reader, are very attached to yours and might even become hysterical with shock, rage, and frustration if anyone tried to keep you from seeing them.

But that's *you*—and *your* feelings count for a heck of a lot more than anyone else's. In fact, they count for everything, and that's precisely why you should feel free to forbid your lover from seeing her friends. It's entirely possible that many of her friends were on board before she met you, so by virtue of seniority, those friends might even believe that they have an equitable claim on your lover's time and attention. Those "friends" (put it in quotes, because what do they count for compared with you?) might even feel that they have a right to criticize and judge you! You heard me right. They might feel that way because they've known your lover since infancy or grade school. Well, that's just plain intolerable.

If you catch even a whiff of such freaking treason (and *treason* is not too strong a word here), you must nip it in the bud right away by simply telling your lover that she's no longer allowed to visit with Bonnie or Karen or whoever it may be. If she starts to pull a long face and sulk, you can just nail her good by screaming that if she wants to associate with people who are trying to sabotage your relationship, you might as well call it quits right then and there!

Now, it would bother you a lot if your lover tried to pull the same thing with you, but as my pal, the eminent investor and shrink, Phil DeMuth, says, "That's someone else's feelings, and only your feelings count." So just steamroll right over your lover's objections, and make sure to control the access she has to any negative input—or even questionable input—about you.

Your goal here is to basically put your lover in a situation similar to that of a person living in a totalitarian state. That level of control will basically make your lover's life easier. She doesn't need to have any discretion or independence of mind. You can start making all of her decisions by just regulating who her friends are and when they can be in her presence. You know what? She'll get used to it. And she'll even thank you eventually—because, hey, you're the boss!

♡

Now, I want to shift gears a tiny bit here. So far, most of this book has been about how to ruin your love life, assuming you already have a relationship that can be ruined. That's well and good, and we all need this advice. But how about some advice for those of you who don't have a relationship yet? How about some tips that will ensure that you will never have a decent relationship—not even for a few months? I, your faithful author, certainly don't want any of you who are not in a relationship to feel as if you're being slighted. So please read on for some advice on how to make sure you never have the chance to develop any kind of decent love life in the first place.

25

Only Pursue Men or Women Who Are Already Taken

Sometimes the best, most powerful advice is the simplest, and that's certainly the case here. How can you make sure that you have the smallest possible chance of actually having a decent love life? Simple, silly: Choose someone who's already married or dating someone else! This will more or less guarantee that you'll have an truly unsatisfactory love life. (I exclude those who are legally married but are in fact separated—let's forget about them for this discussion.)

If you think about it, you'll realize that many of the world's most charming men and women are already hitched. They're often far more delightful to be around than those who are single. But if they're married, you can only be with them for fleeting moments. So they'll truly help you attain your goal of ruining your love life by making sure it's always unsatisfying and lacking in substance.

You might also find it worthwhile to try "dating" someone who's gay and only attracted romantically to his own sex. Once again, these individuals can be thoroughly delightful. And they're often quite good-looking. So go ahead and fall in love with a homosexual if you're a heterosexual (or vice versa). The result is almost sure to be a maddening period of frustration and loneliness.

Similarly, why not develop a relationship with someone who's a hopeless workaholic? This isn't as bad as dating someone who's married, but it comes close. The workaholic is married to his *work,* and his relations with anyone and anything *but* his work will always be of a meager and unsatisfying kind. You may very well get him to the altar . . . but that may also be the last you see of him for some time to come.

Or try dating someone who's unavailable because he's still basically having a romantic relationship with his mother or father. There are plenty of these folks around, and you may manage to corral one of them to the altar. But you're going to be stunned by just how little real devotion you get out of this species when push comes to shove and the time for choosing between Mom and Dad on the one hand, and you on the other, comes up.

To be sure, devotion to one's parents is a fine thing, noble and pure. But dating someone in his 20s or 30s or (heaven forbid) older, who still lives with Mom and Pop—well, good luck to you. You're looking for fish in a desert.

There are undoubtedly countless other ways in which people can be unavailable to you—both emotionally and physically (how about falling for a Catholic priest!), and I couldn't possibly list them all here. But the general principle should suffice: If you want to have a relationship that's guaranteed to fail, definitely pursue someone who's already taken!

26

Always Look Your Worst— or at Any Rate, Don't Bother to Look Your Best

Perhaps you've heard the ancient piece of wisdom that "love enters through the eyes . . ." This just implies that men and women fall in love because they like the way the other person looks. And certainly, there's a multimillion-dollar industry in this country alone that says that we should all look our best—the intent being to impress and attract the opposite (or maybe the same) sex.

Men and women go to gyms, sweat, struggle, and torture themselves—all to tone their bodies to optimal fitness. Similarly, people diet, starve themselves, have surgery, buy prodigious amounts of makeup, and purchase the latest fashions—all to make themselves look wonderfully attractive and sexy (at least to themselves).

Well, love comes in through the eyes all right; and the human race, even in the most dire straits of illness, poverty, and war, will always take the time to look good. It's a basic part of the condition of all living creatures (including plants and animals), who go to a lot of genetically engineered effort to look their best to attract mates and continue the species.

But none of this means a thing to you! You can and must look any old way you feel like. It's a law set down in the Commandments that you must only do what's easiest and requires the least effort on your part—and to hell with what other people think. Let your hair be unkempt and greasy. Get fat. Wear dirty clothes. In fact, go to a lot of trouble to make yourself look positively unsightly—not just ordinary, but ugly. Tattoo your entire body. Put hooks and other metal in your face and call it face jewelry. Make yourself look absolutely hideous with this stuff, and call it fashion.

And don't make it easy for the world to *see* the real you. Make them really stretch and struggle to find out just who you are. And don't bother to help them by advertising yourself as attractive. Instead, put your ugly face forward and make them search for that really lovely person who's presumably hidden under the grunge and sweat stains and pimples and grease (the alternative, of course, is that the hideous one *is* the real you, but that's just not possible, is it?).

Those fashion magazines don't know what they're talking about. You can be just as slobby as you want and the world will owe it to you to find the real you. Yes, the world commands that every other human look great and go to a lot of trouble just to get a second glance. But *you* don't have to. In your case, the world will make an exception and like you even better . . . the worse you look.

27

Be Consistently Surly and Unfriendly

This one is so basic that maybe it should be set in glowing neon letters. If the publishers can't arrange that, then just take my word for it—this is the big one, the nuclear bomb of ways to ruin your love life by making sure you don't have one to start with.

You may have noticed that from elementary school—no, from kindergarten—onward, the kids who had girlfriends and boyfriends tended to be the ones who were friendly, outgoing, and pleasant. And in adult life, it's nearly universally true that those who have friends and lovers are the ones who have some manners and are able to make conversation, express some interest in others, and have what we might call a civilized approach to life.

You may have even heard that men and women often make friends first before becoming lovers. This surely is a basic fact of human existence for most people: The friendlier and easier to get along with you are, the better the chance that you'll find a wonderful person who can be your lover.

Yes, this is true for the human race—and even for dogs, cats, and other cute and furry species. But it isn't going to be true for *you*. You can act just as rude and surly as you want. You can be reclusive and unpleasant. You can punctuate your speech with sarcasm and anger. You can stand mute when asked even the most innocuous questions and simply respond with a look of contempt and derision.

And when you behave in this rude way, it's the other person's duty to work through your defenses and your rudeness to find the lovely invisible self that might possibly be lurking beneath all the barbs and thorns.

You say that you're 40 and you've been doing this rude act all of your life and no one has yet bothered to try to penetrate it? Well, then act even ruder. The problem might just be that you're being too nice even though you're not trying to be.

Stand up for yourself! Make it really, really hard for anyone to be your friend or lover. Put up barbed wire. Build minefields. It's the world's duty to get through all of that to find the charming inner you that might (or might not) be lurking there.

Just be sure that you never act friendly, nice, kind, or compassionate—and your love life will take care of itself.

28

Act Like a
Big Baby on Dates

Looking slobby and acting surly should prevent you from having that date in the first place. But let's suppose that someone really does go to the trouble of trying to get through to you. Furthermore, let's say that you get asked out, either on a date or as part of a group, and then you split off with someone who seems to be particularly interested in you.

To make sure that your love life *stays* ruined, act like a big baby on your date by doing all or some of the following:

— *Talk nonstop, and talk only about yourself.* This, by the way, is darned good advice for wrecking any situation, but it's especially good for wrecking a date. Don't ask any questions of your companion. Don't talk about movies or music or art or world affairs. Don't ask her where she's from, where she went to college, what she does for a living, or whether she has any brothers and sisters. Only talk about yourself (without letting her get a word in edgewise, of course), and by all means resist any attempts by your companion to interject discussion on some topic she's interested in. Talk until her eyes glaze over. Talk until all the servers at the restaurant have gone home. Talk like there's no tomorrow. Just talk, talk, talk—and don't listen to one damn thing she has to say! I'll say it over and over: Talk only about yourself, you big lovable ogre.

— *Bitch and complain.* Don't ever say anything positive. Bitch and moan about your work. Whine about your parents. Complain bitterly about your neighbors. Bitch about politics and about the economy. Make sure the person you're with knows that you have a totally dour attitude about life. It will do you a lot of good to always appear down, gloomy, and unsatisfied. People enjoy being around others who are really depressed. So act as glum as you can.

And it's really crucial that you talk non-stop about your health—or lack thereof. Go into excruciating detail about your illnesses—especially reproductive- and digestive-system conditions. Talk about that gross scar running across your abdomen, and oh, don't forget your persistent problem with flatulence. Maybe even provide sound effects. Explain how you don't really need a lover so much as a nurse or doctor. People who barely know you will really want to hear about your diseases, your operations, and your medications. So just talk about all of this as much as possible right off the bat—and you're sure to get a good-night kiss (off).

— *Brag wildly, while at the same time maintaining a completely negative attitude about life.* Tell her how many triumphs you've had at work—or would have if the system wasn't stacked against you. Boast about how cool your comeback was to your boss—until he fired you. Talk about what a great-looking family you come from—except that everyone needed to have plastic surgery to achieve that look.

Bragging is a big way to guarantee that the other person you're with will absolutely never want to see you again. So do it, and be happy with yourself. But if you *are* happy with yourself, act unhappy. Understand? But then you're never happy, so never mind.

— *Go on and on about old lovers.* This is so important that it's worth repeating. I know I already hinted at this earlier in the part about how to ruin existing love relationships. And believe me, it works. But it works just as well if you're trying to ensure that you never have a relationship at all. I'm not going to belabor such a lovely and beguiling point. Let's just say, "Try it. You'll like it." Talk about previous lovers right from the start, and you'll find that you eventually have absolutely no one else to talk to at all.

— *Make alcohol and/or drugs the third partner at each and every social interaction. In fact, show up drunk or stoned for your first date.* If your date indignantly points out that you're intoxicated, just tell her that she should have a few drinks or take a few hits on the bong, too, because "it'll loosen you up." Then, when you go out on your date, get steadily drunker. Or more stoned. This is a certified, dyed-in-the-wool showstopper. Hardly any date can survive if the participants are whacked. Being drunk or stoned leads to lousy interpersonal relationships, arguments, long pauses, uncontrolled giggling, shameless flirting with strangers—virtually a whole special category of ruinous relationship patterns (including, of course, risking killing someone while you're on your date by driving drunk or stoned!).

And here's a very important point: Don't just reserve alcohol and drugs for new beginnings in dating and relationships. Make sure you're drunk or high every time you see or even talk to your lover. Continual inebriation is one of the best ways to wreck even the hardiest of relationships, as the partakers slip into comas of self-obsession, unreality, and obnoxiousness. Count on it. So, make alcohol and drugs your constant companions. It'll work like a charm.

♡

Now let's assume that you followed all of the great advice offered above and did your best to nip the relationship in the bud, but it still didn't work and you somehow managed to start up a relationship.

If that's the case, here are some more suggestions for how to ruin it pronto. . .

29

Take Total Possession of Your Lover's Home

Make sure that your lover knows that you're now in residence and in charge.

If you're a man, leave your clothes around the apartment, and also camp out in the bathroom reading the sports page of *The Times*. If you're a woman, after you've spent a night or two at the apartment of your new lover, leave panties and a big box of Tampax lying around.

Be rude to her friends. Redecorate his place without asking. Eat everything that's in her refrigerator and don't replace it for her. Read his snail mail *and* his e-mail behind his back. Rummage through her closets and drawers. Answer his phone and act really rude to whoever calls—especially if it's his parents. If they seem a bit shocked that a stranger is answering the phone, make lewd innuendoes about the sex you had the night before. Change the message on the machine so that you're on it, either in the background or actually on the outgoing message.

Just assume that your lover's house is now yours, and that you can do any old thing you want in it. Show him who's boss by planting the flag of your possessions in his dwelling. Intrude on the peace and quiet of her home by blasting loud music and by inviting your obnoxious, raucous friends over without asking her.

Remember, your lover's place is now yours (and don't forget to make copies of his keys behind his back). People like to be violated and pushed around in their own personal space, and this will do very well for you. It virtually guarantees a swift end to the relationship (which is what you want, right?).

30

Flirt with Anyone and Everyone— in Front of Your Lover

This is so important that it not only applies to the folks *in* a relationship, but also to those who might be contemplating getting into one, are just starting one, or who are going out on a first date.

First and foremost, flirt with your date's roommate. Yes! Yes! Yessss! Even as your date is getting ready for you, engage in sexual innuendo with the person she lives with—

preferably within your date's earshot. And then once you're out on the date, turn up the flirt-a-thon meter. Flirt with the valet parking attendant. Flirt with the other person's date if you're doubling. Engage in a long conversation with the restaurant hostess, delving into where she's from, what her real job is, how she got to be so cute, and in the meantime, completely ignore your date. Show much more warmth to an old girlfriend you run into than you do to the person you're actually having dinner with.

When you go to the movies, flirt with the gal behind you in line. And then, when your date's in the middle of a sentence, make a big show of turning your head to stare at the good-looking babe who just walked by. Flirt with any and every woman who crosses your path!

Short of having sex with someone else right in front of your date, there's practically nothing else you can do to wound her feelings as deeply and as consistently as flirting with others. It goes right to the core of any relationship and can ruin it immediately. Or even better, it will slowly eat away at it like battery acid for days, weeks, and months (c'mon, no one taking these rules seriously will have a relationship that lasts beyond months!). Flirting with others belittles your lover, makes her feel jealous and insignificant, and keeps her in a state of perpetual anger.

Bottom line: You can't lose in the relationship-killing department by flirting constantly with others in front of your lover. Flirting: It's to relationships what atom bombs are to cities.

31

♡ ♡ ♡ ♡

Make the Decision That You're Going to Marry for Money— and Don't Let Love Enter into the Equation

You may have heard the old saw that the hardest way on earth to earn money is to marry it. That is, you have to kowtow to your spouse's rich family; you have to tolerate their automatic assumption that they're better than you are because their bank account has more zeroes at the end of it, and you have to figure out which fork to use when sitting at their lavish dinner table.

Well, that's all nonsense. Rich people are very friendly and tolerant of poor people who are courting their son or daughter just for their money. They'll love the thought that they're going to be sharing their money with someone who doesn't have a dime. And they'll treat you nicely and even dote on you simply because you're *not* rich.

Yes, and if you believe that, I have an Internet stock to sell you.

The sadder truth just might be that the wealthy will in fact treat you like dirt because *they* are rich and *you* are poor, and this is a fact of life, not to be changed or tampered with by you or anyone else. Rich people want their kids to marry other rich people's kids. The famous phrase, "Rich marries rich," happens to be true, and if you try to tamper with it, you cross an invisible but very painful line of demarcation that will shock you out of your misconceptions.

So go ahead. Do everything possible to marry someone just for money—not for love or contentment or lifelong enjoyment—and I'll guarantee that your life will be rich . . . in misery.

32

♡♡♡♡

If Your Lover Has Parents Who Are Simply Intolerable, Believe in Your Heart That He or She Will Turn Out Totally—or Even a Little Bit—Different from Those Parents

You've probably heard people say that if you want to get a good idea of what your lover is going to look like in 30 years or so, have a gander at her parents. You'll get an eyeful. But there's something much deeper level that you might want to think about. That is, if you want to assess what your lover's personality is going to be like, check out how her parents or older siblings act *now*.

Rarely in this world does the apple fall very far from the tree, and it's not likely that it will in this case either. If you're a man and your lover's mother is materialistic, carping, and complaining, but your lover is a flower child, think about it: Her mother is not going to change into a flower child. But your lover may very well change into Mom—and that's a scary prospect indeed.

If you're a woman and your lover is a robust, hearty sportsman, and his father is a complaining, racist old alcoholic, you may well find that as time goes by, your lover gets to be far more like his father than is comfortable.

If you make your choice based on the firm conviction that your lover will never change, will always be as wonderful as she is now, and will never fall into the gravity of her parents' behavior, you're an astounding optimist, to put it mildly.

But knowing you and how everything always works out for you, you'll probably just go ahead and marry the man or woman with the monsters-from-hell parents. In your case, and *only* in your case, will the apple actually fall *far* from the tree. Good luck!

33

Act Out of Jealousy Any Old Time You Feel Like It; in Fact, Let Jealousy Rule Your Life

You've probably noticed that people don't always make the best decisions when they're motivated by jealousy. In fact, it's almost impossible to think clearly when you're getting whipped around by this most insatiable and evil of personality demons. Jealousy can make even the most sensible woman go berserk, and can make even the most calm of men go shrieking insane.

But don't let that stop you in the slightest in your quest to totally control your lover with this emotion. You're the only person in history who will make the proper decisions while under the influence of the green-eyed monster. You and you alone can make the envy devil your god and still make things work for you.

For example, did you see him talking to another woman in a department store—not in a flirtatious way, but just transacting business? Did you see her smiling warmly to a client as she tried to close the sale of a house?

Freak out! Go crazy on her. Start yelling at him. Throw major fits. Go totally insane with rage (always a good idea when trying to annihilate any relationship anyway). Toss dishes around. Slam doors. Run out the door and swear you're never coming back.

Did you happen to come upon some ten-year-old photos of your lover with an old girlfriend? *Go berserk!* Make him writhe and bend and break with his own hysteria as he cowers from your rage. Spare no wrath. That's for wimps and losers. Pour on all of the fury until you feel as if the blood vessels in your forehead are about to burst.

This is the way to make sure you're absolutely and totally in control—let your own emotions run wild, and trample on the dignity and self-esteem of your lover on a continual basis.

Be sure he knows it's your way—with your hysterical fits of jealousy that can flare up at any time—or the highway. I assure you that things will work out just as you would think.

Bye-bye, love.

34

Trust That First Flush of Love, Affection, and Sexual Excitement— and <u>Know</u> That It Will Last Forever

In that warm glow at 4 A.M., after three bouts of lovemaking, when you're still bursting with excitement that she actually came home with you—that's the time to make long-term plans. Although you've never ended up in a relationship with someone you made love to on the first night you met, you know that *this* time it will be different. In fact, this will probably last forever. So make her a key to your apartment and lend her some money—after all, you'll probably end up marrying this person. Yes, you can bask in that warm glow after your first few episodes of love, and know that this is the woman who will bear your children or the man who will care for you in your old age.

You can have faith in that first blast of fireworks. It will light up the sky of your love forever, and your dazzling opinion of your lover will never change. After all, the more you know about people, the more you admire them—isn't that the way it works? And don't lovers always look better in the morning?

This is so obvious that I think I'll just let it go at that.

35

Develop an Intense Relationship with Someone with Severe Personal Problems, and Believe in Your Heart That You Can Change Him

That's right. If your lover has mind-blowing personal problems that seem to be totally unfixable, don't worry. *You* can fix those problems. You and you alone can change human personality so that your lover becomes more honest, more caring, more selfless. You have that magic power that only genies usually have to alter people's behavior. You'll be just as powerful as Jahweh was with Moses near the burning bush. You'll be the lightning bolt in his life that changes him into exactly the person you want him to be.

In fact, this leads to an equally powerful rule: If you start a relationship with someone who has horrific problems, continue with that relationship indefinitely, because he'll most certainly change into the person you want him to be *in time.* Don't give up. Just stay with the loser forever, and he will eventually—through the chemical magic of your strong personality—become a shining star.

Is he a liar? So what? *You* will turn him into the next George Washington. Is he a shirker and a slacker? Never mind. Your relentless nagging will transform him into Bill Gates. Is he constantly unfaithful? So what. If you stay with him forever and devote your life to that cause, maybe by the time you're 70 he'll understand the concept of fidelity.

Remember, people do change—but only for you—and only if you love them with all your heart.

36

Have an Affair with Your Lover's Best Friend or Roommate, and Trust That She'll Never Find Out or Even Care!

You know she's been eyeing you. Go for it! Flirt with her, then get her drunk and have sex with her. Your girlfriend won't find out. No way. She'll just go on with her life and work and will probably be too preoccupied to even care when her roommate comes into her room and says, "I have a terrible confession to make. I'm so sorry. Boo-hoo."

And then, when the confession about your making tacos together is out in the open, your lover will just casually tell her roommate (with a smile), "Oh, that Johnny, he's a wild man. He's totally insane. What a character. Listen, I have a lot of work to do. Could you leave me alone for a while?" (While she gets out the butcher's knife.) No, really, lovers don't care if you have sex with their best friends. Just go ahead and do it (I mean, "do" *her*) and live it up while you're at it.

You and you alone can betray your lover with someone close to her and get away with it. Go ahead! Live dangerously! Have a good time. It'll be something you can tell your grandchildren. People like to be surprised by things that will jolt them to their very core.

So just go for it, have a great time, and you'll soon be having fun and laughing like mad with your lover once again—money-back guarantee (you've heard about Winning Ben Stein's Money, right?).

37

Pretend to Be Someone You're Not

Pretend to be rich if you're poor. Pretend to be socially prominent even if you're a nobody. Pretend to be a total superstar, and keep up the illusion as long as you possibly can.

Pretend you're tough when you're weak. Pretend you're a filmmaker when you're a sales clerk. Just pretend constantly, and soon enough, it will all work out, and you'll be in hog heaven, pretending to be what you're not even a little bit.

Your lover will delight in discovering that the person she's dating is a total phony. She'll love finding out that the guy she's been spending the night with has been telling big fat lies about who he is.

Some might say it undermines the basis of the relationship when someone constantly lies. But that's nonsense. Why? Because when you make up a totally phony persona for yourself, it shows how imaginative and clever you are to have been able to keep up that lie for so long. It shows that you're really a magician who can shape reality in whatever way you choose. What an amazing talent!

Don't buy into that b.s. about how people don't like to be lied to. You can do any old thing you want any old time you want and get away with it, as long as you're charming in your wildly amusing duplicity.

38

Get Involved in Your Lover's Family Business

You heard me right. Insinuate yourself into your lover's family business as thoroughly and as quickly as possible. Don't worry that this will create problems and complications that you couldn't have even conceived of. Just get a big bowl and toss in jealousy, competition, financial conflicts, personality quirks, and family secrets—and watch that old pot boil. What fun you'll have!

Some may say that things might erupt because other employees (or family members) will be jealous of you, and maybe they'll be suspicious that you won't have to work as hard as everyone else, but that's silly. Some might also say that there will inevitably be a problem if you combine the intricacies of (future or current) in-laws, work, and love together. But that's nonsense, too. No, you will be able to make it all work. So just embroil yourself in the inner business workings of your lover's family—and see what happens! Chances are, you'll end up with one very happy soufflé of good cheer, insouciance, and lifelong prosperity.

And the French are our best friends!

39

Believe in Your Heart
That There's Always
Someone Better Just
Around the Corner, and
Treat Your Current Lover
Like He or She Is Merely
a Temporary Substitute for
the Real Thing

If you're a woman, steal a look at your current lover. Is he as good-looking as Brad Pitt? As muscular as Arnold? As smart as your most erudite college professor? As rich as a Rockefeller?

If you're a man, is she as lovely as Ashley Judd? As well paid as Oprah Winfrey? As sexy as Nicole Kidman? If you answer in the negative, then why the heck are you bothering with this person? All you have to do is keep in mind that your current lover can and will be replaced at the drop of a hat by someone else who might be sexier, richer, better connected, and have a better figure.

Always express reservations about your lover, too, and never commit fully—because you know that there's someone much better right around the bend. By keeping your lover guessing, you can ensure that he'll also be in that fragile state of insecurity that will keep him on his toes. And you'll also want to be on *your* toes—so that you're ready to pounce on that golden boy who's ready to plop down right in your lap.

Now when you run a relationship with these things in mind, you'll also be tempted to start fights, throw fits, flirt with others, and fail to be there totally on an emotional level. That will definitely keep you from experiencing the kind of contentment that might lead to a satisfactory and long-lasting love life. Always waiting for something better to come along and never appreciating what you have in the moment will most certainly help your relationship blow up like a torpedo hitting a rusty old freighter.

40

Act Morally Superior to Your Lover

Make sure he knows that you're above him in the eyes of the Lord. If he eats meat, become a vegetarian. If he hunts, then avert your eyes from what he brings home and sob.

And for you men, if she applies eye makeup, make sure you let her know that it was tested on innocent rabbits. If she's watching a soap opera, make sure she's aware that the sponsor's commercials feature detergents that have been tested on little kitties.

At all times, let your lover know that you're on the straight runway to heaven, while he's going straight to hell. People like to be told they're morally inferior, and you'll get an immediate bang for your buck by letting your lover know that you're above him in terms of the rules and strictures of your faith—or of humanitarianism, generally. Keep him feeling low, and he'll really thank you for it.

41

Make Up Strict Rules of Conduct to Keep Your Lover Under Total Stalinist Control

Make up rules about what he's allowed to eat—supposedly, of course, for his own good. Don't let him eat the foods he really likes. They'll kill him! Only your homeopathic brew will save him, no matter how tasteless it is.

And don't let him spend much time watching his favorite sports on TV. They're a waste of time in your eyes, and therefore punishable by time in the no-affection gulag if he violates your dictum.

As for her, berate her for reading her favorite trashy novels, and make her feel guilty about it if she does. And be sure she doesn't spend time chatting with her friends on the phone (even though it's so much fun), because it violates rules about spending time constructively.

The great Roman known as Cato the Censor had a rule that slaves on his estate were only allowed to work, eat, or sleep, and nothing else. This is the way it should be with your lover. Keep him regimented and under your control. I mentioned this before in terms of regulating his social life, but be especially strict about everything I've mentioned here . . . and you'll be sure to see dramatic results.

42

Avoid Developing Any Common Interests

Just do your own thing and scoff at your lover's interests. Don't make any effort whatsoever to spend time with her as she does the things she loves.

Don't stay up late watching her favorite old movies with her. Don't walk the dog with her at night. (In, fact, don't even *have* pets, which might constitute a shared interest.) Don't have stimulating conversations around the dinner table where you discuss world events, people you know, or your respective families. What's the point?

Just go your own way, and make sure she knows that you don't give a damn what she cares about or the things she wants you to do with her. You have your own life, after all, and shared interests are for weaklings. You're a mighty and powerful being who has the right to do your own funkadelic thing anytime you want, any way you want.

Common interests? Ixnay.

43

Don't Value Your Lover's Achievements

So what if he just got a raise? Lots of people get raises. So what if he just won a prize in his art class? His work will never be in a museum. Don't let your lover's pitiful little triumphs go to his head. Just keep at him to do better—or else, even better, just ignore him and let his pride wither on the vine. Yes, if you do something modest and decent, *you* expect lavish praise, of course. But when your lover does something estimable, just freaking ignore it now and forever.

People don't need praise and recognition. Or if they do, what business is that of yours? You need only worry about your own praise, not anyone else's. Keep that straight and it will do you a lot of good.

And who cares if it doesn't do anyone else any good? Who counts in this world? You, and that's it.

44

When Things Are Going Really Well, Start a Fight

Think about it for a moment. When things are going really well, isn't that exactly the time when things are a bit . . . um . . . boo-rring? I mean, where's the excitement in just sitting contemplatively with your lover or lying with your bodies intertwined in silence? Where's the joy in that? You want to know the answer? There isn't any!

I'll say it again: Happiness and peace and quiet are boring. No, what you need is excitement and anger and violence and drama. So, start that fight right now. You can always find a reason.

The bathroom's a mess. The toothpaste tube isn't straightened out. The toilet seat was left up. Your black sock got lost in the dryer. There are plenty of reasons to fight if you really look for them. I mean, make up a reason if you need to.

That's it. Get the blood boiling and the juices flowing. Fight, fight, fight. That's the ticket. Now you're talking: Fight, argue, spar, scream, yell, rant, rave—no one can say you have a tired love life now. And brag to all your friends about how much fun it is to make up after a good bout with your lover.

That's right. You know that the best thing you can do for your relationship is to stir things up.

I won't bother to argue this point anymore.

I think you get it.

♡

That's it. Those are the rules.
Now go ahead, you knucklehead.
Go out there and ruin your
love life . . . or save it.

♡♡♡♡

AFTERWORD

♡♡♡♡

I know what you're thinking, you devil. You're saying to yourself, "Hey, don't tell a soul, but I make a lot of those mistakes in my own life. I sure hope no one notices." Well, unfortunately, not only can you be totally sure that someone notices, you can be sure that *everyone* notices.

Most of all, the people you're in love with will take note of your behavior—that is, if you have the *capacity* for love. If you don't, then nothing I've written here can help you.

As you read this book, perhaps you'll say, "Hey, I guess I really do sometimes ask my lover to work for me without expressing gratitude for it." Or maybe you'll acknowledge, "Gee, I suppose I do play phone games and throw tantrums," and

"Ha! Maybe I do make fun of my lover's family in front of other people." Or perhaps late at night while you're watching TV in the den you'll suddenly acknowledge, "Well, I guess I really do act as if making love to my mate is a chore."

In fact, unless you're a perfect human being (and who is), you're almost sure to recognize some (or many) of the ruinous characteristics that are laid out in this book.

The simple idea here is: "STOP DOING IT, YOU FOOL!" When you find yourself starting fights over nothing, when you notice that you're always sulking and not telling your lover why, when you realize you're trying to control your lover's life, when you realize you never say "I love you" . . . start behaving in a new and better way. People *can* change. Maybe others can't make them change, but they can change. And if you don't want to be sad and lonely for the rest of your life, you *must* change. (By the way, make sure the change is well under way before you get married, and that it's appreciated. . . .)

People rarely do, in fact, *totally* change, but if they're given an absolutely clear road map, they can modify their behavior somewhat, and if you want to know how to start, here's a clue: Get up off the wrong track, start to make changes right now, and do the very best you can. This advice was given to me long ago by the great editor, Jim Bellows, and it's advice worth heeding: *Start right now, and do the best you can.* Love is a job—albeit a wonderful job—and you have to apply yourself to make it work. But if you *do* work at it, the pay is fabulous.

♡♡♡♡

How to Ruin Your Financial Life

1

$ $ $

Forget about Tomorrow

How many of you remember that great old 1950s song called "Forget Domani"? It basically advised the listener to forget about "tomorrow" (*domani* in Italian) and just live for today.

Well, that's what you should do, too—forget about tomorrow. That's right. It's always today. Tomorrow will never come at all, so don't make any plans for the future. Making plans is a lot of work, and thinking about the future is frightening. It's a lot easier to just think about today.

Plans for the future involve calculations and variables and may require some form of selfdiscipline—yuck. Plus, there's so much uncertainty about the future that sometimes you don't really feel good when you think about it. So why think about it at all? It's just a way to get prematurely gray. Instead, think about what fun you can have now, and how much enjoyment and spending you can cram into one day.

And do not make any financial plans— oh no. Forget about making any deposits to a savings account or an Individual Retirement Account (IRA) or a Keogh. Those things are for people who worry about money and end up making themselves sick.

I mean, come on, tomorrow will be just like today. You have enough to eat today, right? You have enough to wear, you own a car, and you have a roof over your head, don't you? Well, then, you'll always be so fortunate because that's just the way things tend to work out in your life.

There's a famous weather-forecasting rule that says that 60 percent of the time the weather tomorrow will be like the weather today. And that's how it will be in your financial life. That means: Don't worry yourself about it. And, oh, that other 40 percent? That will be even *better* than the weather today. Which brings us to the next rule . . .

2

$ $ $

Know with Certainty That There Will Never Be Any Rainy Days in Your Life

There's a lot of talk among old people about saving for a rainy day. You may even have parents or grandparents who lived through the Great Depression of the 1930s or the terrible recession and inflation of the 1970s. They may tell you that things won't always be great economically. There could be a recession, or a new inflation or deflation, or a real-estate collapse, they'll say. You could lose your job. It happened to them, after all. That's why, they'll tell you, you need to put aside money for "a rainy day."

The only problem with this admonition is that it doesn't apply to you. There will be no rainy days in *your* life. Whatever you have now in terms of work, housing, and savings, you will always have. Those bad old days of economic uncertainty are long, long gone. Now we live in a sunny haze of certainty and security. The government's brilliant financial analysts have learned to manage the national economy so that there can never be another really bad economic downturn.

Or, if there is one, it will only last a few days.

On a more personal level, it's just a waste of your good time to consider the possibility of a recession or layoffs at work. These things will simply never happen, and if you plan for them, then you will have penalized yourself by saving money, and not splurging on that vacation or new car you wanted.

Just go on with your life knowing that all is fundamentally well, and that the bad things that happened to other people in other eras will simply never happen to you. It's that basic. You don't need to make any plans for economic security because your life will never have any downs, only ups.

And anyway . . .

$ $ $

Remember That Your Peace of Mind Is a Lot More Important Than the Few Pennies You'll Save Worrying about Money

Let's face it. It's a bit upsetting to think about money. It involves mathematics, and maybe you were never very good at math. It involves discussions of the future, and as we've already come to realize, those discussions can be supremely boring and frightening . . . plus, they're irrelevant to you because it's already been decided that your future is going to be just like your past, only better. When you think about money and the months and years ahead, you have to ponder such things as growing older and the possibility of not having a job—and these are definitely distressing thoughts.

Not only that, but if you start thinking about the future and your financial situation, you might come to the realization that you'll have to make some changes in your life. This might require some self-denial. That's a lot like dieting or exercise—only worse. And that makes it painful to think about.

So, do yourself a favor. Just don't think about saving money—or planning for the future—at all. Go on with your daily routine of life, happy as a clam, content with what you're doing, and don't change a thing. You're calm right now, so why disturb the peace by torturing yourself with worries and plans and financial portfolios and savings accounts? Simply put all that out of your mind.

4

$ $ $

Save Money Only When You Feel Like It, and If You Just Don't Feel Like Saving, Then Don't!

After all, what is saving? It's taking money from present consumption and putting it in a dark vault where you don't have access to it and can't spend it at will. But think about it: What's the good of money if it's hidden away like that? It will just get cold and lonely. But in *your* hands, if you can spend it on something you really enjoy, that money is hard at work making you happy. Sure, you could put the money in a savings account or a CD and it might show up every month as a typed entry on a piece of paper, but what fun is that? It's way better to spend, spend, spend and live it up—and maybe meet a cute guy or gal in the process.

You *could* invest your money in a stock-market account, but then every month you'd get a statement that's complicated and hard to understand. Some months it would show that you were up, and some months you'd be down. (And what a drag it would be to open up that envelope and see you've lost some of your hard-earned cash! You're better off not having that account at all!)

But if you buy several new cashmere sweaters or a new set of golf clubs, you can use and enjoy them right now. And you'll never open a monthly statement that says your Fair Isle sweaters and Big Bertha clubs have gone down the tubes!

Besides, saving is such an abstract concept that involves all kinds of vague notions about uncertainty and the future. Whereas a trip to the Bahamas is real and warm and sunny—and will give you memories for a lifetime.

So spend as much as you can, right here and now. Live for the moment!

5

$ $ $

Don't Bother to Learn Anything at All about Investing

Life is short—far too short to spend your free time reading some dusty old tome on investing your money. Who does that kind of thing anyway? Nerds and worrywarts, and goofy guys with Coke-bottle glasses and pens in their pockets. You're *far* too cool to even think of poring over books with charts and graphs and explanations of why stocks are sometimes better than bonds, and bonds are sometimes better than stocks. Who needs that kind of stuff? Not a hotshot party animal like you who can stay up till 3 A.M. drinking vodka martinis and still be at work at 8! Not someone who has the youth and vitality and smarts that you do.

Leave all that reading and researching non-sense to cranky old folks who have nothing better to do with their time. As for you, you have to get down and get funky. You have to know about J. Lo's latest movies and whether her latest romance with Ben Affleck is working out. These are the things that count in your life.

Plus, you have fascinating TV shows to watch, stomach crunches to do so you can stay in shape, and important phone calls to make to your buddies from college. I mean, what's important? *The National Enquirer* and the latest scoop on what really happened on *The Bachelor,* or devastatingly dull statistics on interest rates?

I think you know the answer to that one.

6

$ $ $

Spend As Much As You Want, and Don't Be Afraid to Go into Debt

What does that mean? It means that in *your* case, and only in your case, you need not pay any heed to balancing income and outgo. Or, in other words, spend as much as you feel like spending and don't worry about it.

For most people and most situations, there has to be some sort of cause and effect. Or so the old folks say. If you eat a lot, you get fat. If you eat a little, you get thin. If you spend more than you earn, eventually you go broke. If you spend less than you earn, you can and do save. If you save a lot, eventually you get rich.

These seem like simple truths. But maybe they're just a bit *too* simple. Do those supposed "truths" take into account that you look really great in that hand-tooled leather jacket? Or that if you buy that new car you'll be the envy of everyone at work? Do those rules take into account that you're a living, breathing guy or gal with blood and heart and desires? Heck, no!

If you see something for sale that you want and need (like that 50-inch plasma TV), you have to buy it whether it puts you into the red or not. After all, life is short and you have to enjoy every minute of it.

Now, what about those people who would try to rain on your parade and say, "Hey, you can't just get further and further into debt"? Well, what about them? Isn't the federal government chronically in debt? It seems to just stay that way year after year, yet no one thinks the federal government is going anywhere. Anyway, there are always people sending you letters offering to lend you money, right? There are always new credit cards arriving in the mail. So what's the problem?

Why do you have to be any different from our esteemed government? If they want a new highway or a new aircraft carrier, they get it, right? Well, *you* want a new bracelet and a trip to Vegas. Maybe both you and the government have to go into debt over it, but so what? Just go for it right here and now, and damn the debt! Win the war to be hip, and then worry about your debts later. In fact, worry about them "tomorrow," because as we've already mentioned, tomorrow never comes!

7

$ $ $

Set Up a High-Profile, High-Consumption Lifestyle with Enormous Fixed Expenses That You Can't Afford

What is life all about? In a few words, looking good to yourself and to others. "To Look good" is probably as short and sweet a reason for why men and women were put on the planet as I've ever heard. I think it was a character in an F. Scott Fitzgerald story who said that the goal of life was to ". . . live fast, die young, and leave a good-looking corpse. . . ." Sounds logical to me. And if looking good is the best thing in life, "feeling good" might be a close second.

It looks good to have a great car. And it makes you happy. So what if the car costs a fortune, your monthly payments are outrageous, and you barely earn enough to pay your rent?! You have to look good no matter what you earn. In fact, you have to look even better if you *don't* earn a lot of money so that people around you will *think* you're doing well. That's where fancy cars, designer clothes, and Pilates all come into play. They make you look good, and that's what counts both on the inside and the outside. That matters a lot more than penny pinching. So what if buying that golf cart overdraws your checking account? It makes you look awfully sharp on the course—and you can always charge it and pay for it over many years—all for a trifling 18 percent interest.

Being cool really comes down to this: High school never ends. And who were the coolest kids in high school? The ones with the best toys. Now it's still high school, whether you're 25 or 55, and you're still really only making the scene if you have the hippest clothes, the newest car, and have just returned from the most elite vacation spot. And if some Scrooge-like accountant warns you that you're overdoing it, tell him to stuff it. After all, life is short. You have to go for it with all the gusto you can right now. Party hearty, dude!

And here's something else to think about: If there's one thing you can be certain of as your expenses mount, it's that one of the most enjoyable things in the whole world is to have a magnificent home. The feeling you get when you walk into a stately mansion or ocean-view condo is one of deep pride and inestimable joy. Plus, people drive by your home and envy you. They ooh and ahh—and isn't arousing the envy of other people one of the best ways to spend money—even if you can't afford to?! What better use is there for money than to make you feel like a big shot? And so what if it makes your friends secretly hate you? At least they're impressed, right? At least they're paying attention to you.

So go even further into debt to set up that high-profile, exorbitantly expensive lifestyle by purchasing the home of your dreams. But wait—there's more, as the TV pitchmen say! Once you've bought the house, don't just let it look like some college dorm room. No! Make sure it's furnished extravagantly. Hire a decorator. If possible, choose the same interior designer that some of the truly rich and famous people have used so that you can brag about *that,* too. To heck with the cost! Did Napoleon worry about the cost when he was building his palaces? Does Bill Gates worry about the cost of his lakefront house? No, and neither should you if you want to make the right impression.

Save money and live within your means? Ridiculous.

But impress your friends and make them seethe with jealousy over your opulent lifestyle? Priceless.

8

$ $ $

Compete with Your Friends to See Who Can Spend the Most

Perhaps I was too harsh in the preceding essay when I talked about arousing the envy and ire of your friends by flaunting that opulent lifestyle you can't really afford. Maybe, rather than doing that, you should set up a friendly little competition to see who can spend the most. For example, take your friends out to a really expensive restaurant and pick up the tab. Then dare your friends to take you to a comparable establishment and eat and repeat—that is, start the whole cycle again, all the while steadily increasing the amounts you're spending on yourself and them (the one with the most expensive lobster wins!).

Or maybe you should compete to see who can take the most expensive vacation. Or who can stay at the most elaborate and pricey hotels. If you really want to, you can set up a situation where you and your friends get sucked more and more into spending money you don't have—until you're all commiserating over your respective bankruptcies.

But don't worry about that now—it's fun to go for broke with your friends. The bigger the risk, the more fun you'll have!

9

$ $ $

Don't Balance Your Checkbook or Keep Track of What You Spend

Why should you? The bank will send you a little form if you're overdrawn, won't they? In the meantime, you'll want to avoid that uncomfortable feeling of being hemmed in by lots of numbers and columns of figures, and instead, just do what's fun and easy.

After all, you're not a machine. You can't be programmed to function like a human calculator. You need to be your own sweet, carefree self.

Besides, if you keep track of how much you spend, it might depress you.

So please don't do it.

10

$ $ $

Forget to Pay Your Taxes

If you're self-employed, which many people are these days, then by all means do not pay your estimated quarterly taxes. It's a lot of bother to do all those computations, and even more of a drag to take money out of your account just to send it in to the government. Why does the government need the money anyway? They already have trillions. And they have legions of employees and office buildings, and lots of aircraft carriers and submarines. They do not need your few measly pennies. They don't care about you!

If the IRS does somehow track you down, demanding the money you owe them, then borrow a line from the immortal Steve Martin and say, "Hey, I forgot." What can they do? It's not like you're an ax murderer. You simply "forgot" (wink, wink) to pay your taxes. This is America, after all. What can they really do to you for not paying up? It's not like this is North Korea or Iran or something. This is a free country, and people are expected to cheat on their taxes—or not pay them at all if they don't want to. And really, who needs the cash more—you or Uncle Sam?

Now, here's another important point: If you have your taxes deducted from your paycheck every pay period, take the maximum number of deductions you can. Claim 12 exemptions even if you don't have any children. Then, when it comes close to April 15, just don't file your income taxes at all, period. That way you get to keep all of that extra money that wasn't withheld from your paycheck. It'll take years, maybe decades, for the IRS to catch up with you. And when they do, at most they'll just smack your hand and give you a big frown. They won't charge you immense interest and penalties. They won't seize your house and your boat and your car. They'll just say, "Well, pay when you can. We understand."

That's the IRS for you. The soul of compassion and forgiveness. Basically, this is an anti-tax country, from the President on down, so live that way and enjoy all that extra money that would have just been wasted by the government anyway.

Another great idea is to use tax shelters to avoid paying your taxes. That's right. Just by paying your accountant and/or your lawyer to draw up some papers and shifting some accounts around, the IRS will be completely fooled, and you won't have to pay a dime. And these things always work. Wait, what's that? You say you read in the newspaper about some tax shelters the IRS cracked down on and the courts invalidated? And you heard about people who had to pay back taxes in the hundreds of thousands and even millions? Well, that was them and this is you. *Your* tax shelters will be perfect and will hold water forever just because they're yours!

An added bonus: If you do get involved with litigating against the government over back taxes, you'll be amazed by how little tax lawyers charge. These attorneys will practically *give* away their services to you, and the fees and expenses will be comically low. And know that the IRS is not at all tenacious. Once they initiate a case, they'll ask you to pay your taxes a few times and then if you don't, they'll just give up and go on to the next guy.

Try it. You'll see. The IRS really just wants to be loved, same as you and me.

11

$ $ $

Truly Believe That You're Only As Valuable As What You Own

Look, this book is just between you and me, right? It's not as if anyone can read your mind and know what you're thinking. So, just between us, even though you're overweight, have a lousy job, and are miserable in your relationship, you know how to make yourself feel empowered, don't you? You know how to build your self-esteem. You know that the way to feel like a superhero is to buy the right things so you can feel great about yourself. You may be short and plump, but your sports car is always the right size. You might feel kind of threadbare on the inside of your soul, but your house is ornate—decorated with money you don't have.

You might be convinced that your friends are all secretly laughing at your failings (and maybe they are, tee-hee), but they won't laugh when they see you pull up in your ultra-cool new Jag sporting your new Rolex (that you charged at 12 percent interest). They'll think you're the last word in chic.

That's just how life goes, isn't it? I mean, no one really likes you—and you don't even like yourself that much—*if* you don't own the coolest stereo, the biggest flat-screen TV, and the most elegant luggage. This is a material world, and you—to coin a phrase—are a material girl . . . or guy. You can't expect to be liked for yourself—it's what you own that determines your self-worth . . . and your worth in the eyes of others.

So put yourself on that treadmill to oblivion. Spend and spend and spend . . . so you can own and own and own . . . and puff yourself up to the point where you finally feel proud of yourself.

You may have heard that happiness is an inside job. Baloney! Happiness comes from getting and spending. Happiness comes from piling up boxes and boxes of things you'll never use. Tommy Hilfiger, Von Dutch, Kate Spade, Armani, Gucci,

Hermès, Mercedes-Benz, Ritz-Carlton—brands and labels are what matter, not self-esteem or a hard day's work or having loyal friends.

You're a nobody—in your own eyes and in the eyes of others—unless you buy and own every cool product and service out there . . . and don't you forget it.

12

$ $ $

Collect As Many Credit Cards As You Can, and Use Them Frequently

You're a citizen of an industrial first-world nation! You're a member of the ruling class. That means that you're entitled to have credit cards—lots of them. And why are credit cards named as such? Because, silly, they allow you to go on credit and buy things you otherwise couldn't afford!

Again, you're a 21st-century citizen! Credit is your right. More than that, going on credit is your civic *duty!* Yes, fellow citizen, what do you think would happen to this glorious nation if you stopped charging goods on your cards? It would be a disaster. Tens of millions of workers would be laid off. Corporate profits would vanish and the stock market would crash permanently. It would be as if a foreign invader had attacked and conquered this great land.

If you don't use your credit cards, you might as well be an agent of Al Qaeda. Well, maybe it's not that bad, but it's close.

So, don't be a saboteur of this nation we all love so much. Borrow, borrow, borrow, and spend, spend, spend. Remember that the credit card is your ticket to ride. It's your rocket ship to the moon. You're just not yourself without a wallet full of cards. You don't feel as if you have "The Power" without them—after all, doesn't some commercial tell you not to leave home without them? If you were limited to just spending what's in your pocket or in your checking account, you'd be cut off at the knees. And we don't want that to happen.

What is the one bold stroke through which you can help out the entire nation and at the same time make yourself feel empowered? Simple: Collect as many credit cards as you can, and max them out.

And then . . .

$ $ $

As Soon As You've Succeeded in Maxing Out Your Credit Cards . . . Get New Ones!

Credit-card application forms come in the mail every day. Make sure you fill out every one of them and acquire as many cards as you can. Don't even try to relate your income to your use of credit cards or your possession of them. Doing so would be madness. Don't try to make your life into a flow chart. I already told you, you're not a machine. Just get the cards and use them to buy what makes you feel good. This isn't just selfishness (as good as selfishness is), it's patriotism.

By the way, do you want to know a good test of whether or not you've overused your credit cards and are carrying too large a balance? Well, if the banks and credit-card companies are still offering you applications for cards, that shows that everything's fine and you have plenty of reserve spending capacity.

See, the credit-card companies have a supercomputer buried in the Utah desert under thousands of feet of concrete. Its purpose is to take care of you and help you out. It monitors your credit-card use, and if it finds that you're using too much credit, it cuts you off in terms of new solicitations. This might seem like a rumor or an urban myth, but it's not. The fact is that the credit-card companies only want what's best for you—really. If they send you new credit cards, that means that you *need* new credit cards (as determined by that supercomputer) and that you can easily handle the load, so fill out those applications, mail them out, and watch the credit cards pour in.

And, closely related to this important directive is the following rule . . .

14

$ $ $

When You Get Your Credit-Card Bills, Pay Only the Minimum Each Month

You'll be pleasantly surprised to see just how little your minimum payment is when you get your credit-card statement each month. In fact, you can charge hundreds of dollars and the minimum will just be a paltry sum. You can charge *thousands* and your minimum might be as little as $100.

How can this be anything but great? I mean, why take on a burden you don't have to take on? And those late fees and finance charges—those items in small print that are listed at the bottom of your statement—well, what about 'em? Why should they get in the way of your having a good time? They'll never amount to much. So what if it takes you 20 years to pay off a $1,500 balance? As long as you're only making $20 payments each month, why bother thinking about how much the credit card company is making off you?

So, just pay the minimum and see how much your financial situation improves!

15

$ $ $

Know in Your Heart of Hearts That You Will Never Run Out of Money

You see, there *is* a good witch, like the one in *The Wizard of Oz*. The good witch makes sure that nothing bad will ever happen to you when it comes to money. This means that no matter how wildly you overspend, you'll never run out of cash. Never.

Well, maybe it's not a good witch, but it's somebody—maybe a father, a mother, a rich uncle, a fairy godfather—someone. And he or she is there to make sure you'll never have to file for bankruptcy or live on the streets.

So what if you can't readily identify someone in your family or social circle who will always bail you out or keep you from experiencing catastrophic financial losses? Don't worry about it. There *is* an invisible someone, somewhere who's looking out for you. You're immune from the fate that befalls those unfortunate others who lose their jobs, blow their trust funds, or bet the house on one hand in Vegas. You have that guardian angel. Those bad things can't happen to you. You're special. You'll always have plenty of moolah to spare. Plenty. And a good fairy sprinkling money all over you.

Count on it.

16

$ $ $

Repeat After Me: "I Am Not Responsible for My Financial Well-Being"

Well, why *should* you take on that responsibility? That would involve (again) a good deal of self-restraint, self-discipline, and abstinence when it comes to buying everything you've always wanted. If you *were* responsible for your own finances, then you'd have to sit down with a calculator and a pad of paper and figure out what you could no longer afford. And that means that you might have to deny yourself on occasion.

Well, that's just plain wrong and shouldn't happen!

So, just go on thinking that someone else will always take care of you (a husband, a wife, a mother, a father, a brother or sister or friend); or that your financial situation is the fault of George W. Bush or the globalists or the Council on Foreign Relations or your local mail carrier. It's never *your* fault no matter what happens to you, and you shouldn't have to discipline yourself—not now or ever. What kind of life would that be? A "fun" life? A life like you see in *Vogue* or *Esquire?* I don't think so, do you?

Responsibility about money is for nerds and geeks. You're a hippie, a free spirit, not an accountant. So do whatever you feel like doing, and let someone else worry about it.

17

$ $ $

Trust That There's Always More Money Coming In

Suppose you get a bonus at work. Some idiots might say that you should save it in case you really need it someday. But why? First of all, I already told you not to save, because that means you're not buying everything you want and need *right now*. But second, just because you got that one bonus, that doesn't mean there won't be another one coming along. So spend that bonus on a vacation or a boat or a new truck! You won't ever get fired. You won't ever get laid off. There will always be tons of money coming in for you to blow on toys and games.

Or, what if you get an inheritance? Great for you, I say. But for heaven's sake, don't be a stingy guy or gal and hoard it. No, the people who left it to you want you to have fun with it. That means go out and spend it.

What's that, you say? It's probably the only inheritance you'll ever get and you'd better sock it away? Uh, I don't think so. I think it would be much more prudent to spend it like a drunken sailor and have faith that somewhere out yonder there's some other generous relation who's also going to leave you a chunk of change. So please don't worry that there will ever be a lack of money—it will never happen!

Where might you get that chunk of change you might need? Well, can you spell L-O-T-T-E-R-Y?

18

$ $ $

Lend Money to Your Friends—Especially Your Girlfriend or Boyfriend

Remember that line from *Hamlet* where Polonius said: "Neither a borrower nor a lender be"? Well, maybe that made sense 400 or so years ago when Shakespeare wrote it, but it's a bunch of baloney today.

Lending money is a good thing. As you well know, lending money binds you together with your friends. It keeps them close. It says that you care. Plus, it shows that you have enough confidence in yourself to part with the money. And most of all, lending money to your friends lets them know that you trust them to pay you back.

And this is true in spades when it comes to your significant others! You want to show them you care, so naturally you'd want to lend them money. This is a genuinely kind thing to do, and it will make them love you even more than they do now. When they pay you back—as they inevitably will—you'll thank them profusely, they'll be eternally grateful, and you'll be even better friends and lovers—even more so than if you'd given them a diamond necklace or an SUV.

They'll be touched that you parted with the money—if only for a brief moment until you got paid back—and *you* will be heartened that they paid you back so promptly and lovingly.

The beautiful part about all this is that history supports the position that you'll get paid back. Lovers always repay money. Those sad sacks you see on *Judge Judy* who didn't pay back their lovers? They're one in a million. Don't even think about them at all. Love means that you always get paid back, and that your love affair will be even stronger after the transaction is completed.

So go for it, trusted reader. Cement those ties and bind them in granite by lending money to friends and lovers.

19

$ $ $

Learn the Ultimate Rule of Success—Money Spent on Appearances Is the Best Money You Can Spend!

Money attracts money. That's an old and very true adage. But suppose you don't have a lot of money to start with? Well, the only way to fool that old money god is to pretend that you *do* have a lot of cash. That means, very specifically, that you must, must, must dress and drive as if you've got some dough. If you wear Armani or Polo, you'll attract other people who wear those labels. They will no doubt be rich, and somehow just by being in their presence, *you* will get rich, too. Similarly, if you drive a Jaguar or a BMW convertible, *you* will be a magnet for those who drive those cars, and they will make you rich as well.

In other words, look and dress the part, and you'll soon be surrounded by other rich people who will start pouring money down on your little head.

Money spent in this manner is far better than saving could ever be. It is, after all, an investment in your future. Great things happen to people who put on the façade. It's that simple. And for heaven's sake, don't start worrying again about how much anything costs. . . . How many times do I have to spell C-R-E-D-I-T C-A-R-D?!

20

$ $ $

Play Lady—or Lord—Bountiful by Shelling Out Money to Everyone Around You

Do you have some sad-sack friends who are always broke? Good! Then take them out shopping and buy them all of the clothing, accessories, and electronic gadgets they need!

Are a bunch of your pals gathering for lunch? Great! Charge the whole meal on your credit card.

Do you have some neighbors who need some cheering up? Fabulous. Buy them something wildly extravagant like diamond jewelry or a membership to a country club.

Do you know some unfortunate souls who have been laid off from their jobs? Oh, that's so sad. Don't just offer to pay their rent—buy them a car. Show that you're the lord of the manor and the one who has money to burn when your friends are in trouble.

Doing so performs the dual function of helping out with the finances of the unfortunate ones, and also making you feel like a big shot. Who cares if you're only a few hundred bucks behind the poor schlubs yourself? Show off anyway. It'll make you feel better, and that's all that counts. Don't worry about what will happen next month when you can't pay your bills. You're Santa Claus, and it's your job to give and give and give.

And anyhow, who doesn't feel good tossing money around as if it were just so much shredded lettuce? And don't ruin the feeling by worrying about it!

21

$ $ $

Don't Think about Retirement—
It's a L-O-O-N-N-G Way Off

The truth is (and you really need to remember this), that you're young and vibrant no matter how old you might happen to be right now. You might be 20 or you might be 40 or you might be 60, but you're still light years away from retirement. In fact, it's so far down the road that you can't even see it. And you know what? You never *will* be able to see it! Time passes very slowly, and your youth, or relative youth, will go on forever. Plus, medical science is making such amazing strides that you'll be biking 20 miles a day and playing five sets of tennis until you're 100.

So why do you need to think about what you're going to live on when you're old and retired? It ain't gonna happen for, well . . . forever. And you'll be totally prepared when the time comes anyway. How? Well, for one thing, the U.S. government will take care of you. Or your relatives or friends will give you money. Or just by virtue of being 65 years old, somehow money will appear from nowhere even though you never invested in anything and have no savings.

Don't you remember how I told you that someone else is always responsible for you? That's true! So don't you worry about a thing.

Just to summarize: First, you won't ever get old. Second, you won't ever have to worry about money. And third, someone else will always take care of you. It's all too boring to even think about it, so don't. Plus, it's really fun to be old and not have any money. It gives you the opportunity for fantasy and invention and trying new things . . . like poverty.

Retirement? Yawn. It just takes care of itself.

$ $ $

Now, let's change gears a bit. Remember how I told you that you shouldn't save anything or worry about your future? After all, it puts lines on your face.

But what if someone has talked you into worrying about money? What if some fool has made you believe that you should invest in stocks or bonds or an IRA? Well, all right. I guess there are some people who can be talked into anything!

But let me give you a few words of advice if you've actually started to begin some kind of investment plan. This is important, so listen up . . .

22

$ $ $

Choose a Broker Based on His (or Her) Good Looks, Fashion Sense, and Gift of Gab

That's the way to choose a stockbroker! After all, how could he have gotten the money for that nice suit or those handsome cuff links if he weren't a star performer in the investment area? How could he always wear those snazzy Hermès ties if he didn't really know his way around the financial world? And don't you find that good-looking people are almost always well-to-do and tend to be smarter than those who are just average-looking? This means that if you can find a broker who's super attractive and put together, he'll undoubtedly know a lot more about stocks than one who's just an ordinary schmoe.

To put it more succinctly, if your broker's a looker, is nattily attired, and is in the finance business, he's obviously made a ton of money for himself . . . and probably for his clients, too. That means he'll make a lot of money for you as well, and then you'll also find yourself hobnobbing at The Polo Club and The Yacht Club and those other places where he hangs out.

The world of finance is a tricky, complex world, so what you want is someone who's smooth-talking and confident. Your broker has to be able to convince you that he can do great things with your money by putting it in junk bonds and other areas too arcane for you to know about personally.

But please don't make the mistake of asking your broker (or potential broker)—just what kind of education he has. Similarly, it would be rude and tasteless to ask him to give you references from satisfied clients. All you need to see is that he's wearing an Armani suit, a Rolex, and Gucci shoes—and then you can breathe a sigh of relief because you know that your hard-earned money will be in good hands.

Another thing: Don't look for nerds and brainiacs when you're shopping for a broker. They may do very well in the classroom, but they're not going to do at all well in the "real world" where savoir faire, toughness, and street smarts combine to (mysteriously) produce an elegantly coiffed stock-market wizard.

And don't hire anyone old or rumpled or boxy looking, or someone who spends his spare time, say, playing bridge instead of downing martinis and spinning the roulette wheel. Basically, look for someone who could be a *GQ* cover boy—that is, someone like Pierce Brosnan and not, well, like Warren Buffett.

23

$ $ $

Attend a "Free" Financial Seminar, and Follow the Advice They "Sell" You to the Letter

Figure it out. If the people who are putting on these seminars are doing it for free, how bad a deal can it be? And how very sure of themselves they must be to offer their advice gratis and just let the merits of their plans and schemes sell themselves, so to speak. There are super-strict government requirements (aren't there?) regulating who can put on these seminars, so the individuals giving the one you're attending wouldn't have even been allowed to do anything that important unless they'd met the most stringent financial, educational, ethical, and legal standards.

This means that you can trust every single word they say. If they tell you they have a "system" or a "program" that's "guaranteed" to produce immense wealth, then rest assured that the Federal Trade Commission (FTC) wouldn't have allowed them to make those claims unless they were true. I can tell you this for sure because I (your author) used to be a lawyer with the FTC, and I definitely saw the beady eyes of those government gumshoes scanning the horizon for every kind of scam—and the ones they unearthed were shut down instantly.

The same thing happens at the Securities and Exchange Commission (SEC). If you can't trust the federal government to look out for your best interests where securities sales are concerned, you can't trust much, and I pity you. (Remember, these are the same people who scouted out Enron and Global Crossing before they did any damage. Now you can relax.)

So, go on, take that free financial seminar! The organizers are good guys and gals who just want you to be wealthy. Join up with them, have a good time, get rich quick, and then maybe you can have a few drinks with them at their next carnival show—oops, I mean seminar.

24

$ $ $

Make a Point of Watching Those Late-Night Financial Success Infomercials

Are you an insomniac? Maybe you work odd shifts and rarely get to bed before three in the morning, or perhaps you're just a clever dog and know how the world works. There's an old Italian saying that goes something like this: *Money is made at night.* Now, this used to mean that money was often gotten illegally and had to be made while the sun didn't shine and people couldn't see what was going on.

But there's a different meaning these days. Nowadays, real wealth is made by those who wait up until midnight or later and then watch infomercials telling them how to make money. Why are these shows on so late at night? Oh, silly you! Because if they were on in the middle of the day, everyone in the world would watch them and learn all the secrets of making a fortune from nothing, and soon everybody would be taking advantage of those deals. After all, how many gorgeous, pristine homes are there in bankruptcy that you can buy with no money down? If the shows that told you how to acquire them were on at 6 P.M. on CBS, they'd all be snapped up.

So the late bird gets the worm in this case. The late bird gets to stay up late, see what's what in the world of finance, and make real money while all the rest of us lazy slobs are sleeping.

Now, it may seem to you that the people on these shows are a bit vague about how they acquired all those yachts and polo ponies. But that's because, again, the information they're disseminating is classified and is intended only for the eyes and ears of those smart enough to stay up late and watch TV.

Pity those poor fools who think Ben Franklin knew what he was talking about. You know the *real* way to be healthy, wealthy, and wise: Stay up late, pay attention to the "wealth-building program" of the evening, and be happy.

25

$ $ $

Rest Assured That If a Person Is Quoted in *The Wall Street Journal* or on TV, She (or He) Must Be Able to Forecast the Stock Market

It ain't easy to get on TV. Just ask anyone. That means, in a nutshell, that if someone gets on air to talk about the stock market, she must have passed rigorous government and private tests that gauge her ability to predict what's going to happen. The TV shows keep close track of every syllable that she ever says about the market. These words are then compared with how the market actually did. A precise correlation is made on complex graphs and top-secret computers.

Anyone who doesn't live up to very strict standards is immediately bounced right off the airwaves. If, for instance, a stock-market analyst told you that tech stocks were the ticket to wealth and riches back in March of 2000 before the Crash, that person would be immediately banned from all network- and cable-TV news and financial programs. The TV stations and networks have reputations to protect, and they cannot guard those reputations if they don't assiduously check to make sure that every "expert" they put on the air is consistently right.

So rest assured that if someone appears on a TV show and talks about the stock market, you can be very, very certain that she knows what the heck she's talking about, and you'll make jillions just by heeding her advice.

The same is true for the financial press. Magazines and newspapers such as *Fortune* or *Business Week* or *The Wall Street Journal* closely follow every prediction and pontification of every person they quote. This means that they screen carefully for those who have made mistakes in the past and ban them forever from their pages if they've been found wanting. For example, if someone ever said that the stock market was fairly priced when the Dow was 12,000 and was going far higher in the future . . . and then it fell to 7,500 . . . an account would be kept, and those people would not be allowed to dispense any advice in the future. If they said that you should get out of real estate and into stocks when the NASDAQ was about to fall by 80 percent, they would never be called upon for their words of "wisdom" again.

So know that you can abide by the information given by anyone who has ever appeared on TV or in the financial press. These "experts" know what they're doing, and if they didn't, how could they be associated with such prominent broadcast and print organizations?

Yup. They really know their stuff.

26

$ $ $

Don't Pay Any Attention to Financial Experts Who Urge You to Diversify—the Stock Market Is Always the Best (and Only) Place to Be!

Hey, the long-term trend of the stock market is always up, up, and away. I mean, the Dow has risen from about 40 in 1933, to about 9,600 as I write this in 2003, so just look at the curve, man! That doesn't even count dividends. Just a few thousand socked away in the depths of the Great Depression would translate to millions nowadays.

The fact is that all of the smart people know that the long term will bail you out in the stock market and will make you rich. So stay in it and keep adding to it all the time. And whatever you do, don't spread your money around and put it into anything else.

Some mean-spirited, grumpy people such as Alan Abelson (a financial columnist for *Barron's*) might warn you that there have been long periods when the stock market has gone way, way down. They might tell you that even in postwar periods, there have been decades when the stock market hardly moved at all in an upward direction.

Do not believe them! Forget about the crash of 1987. Forget about the disasters in 1973 and '74. Don't pay any attention to the fact that it took the stock market 25 years after 1929 to reach its 1929 level again; or that adjusted for inflation, it took the market more than 50 years to reach its 1929 level again—or that the NASDAQ had the worst stock-market plunge in postwar history just a few years ago.

The people who tell you these things are just party-pooping spoil sports. Don't pay any attention to them. The truth is that all of these little blips may have happened, but they're just tiny eddies and cross-currents in a majestic river flow of progress, prosperity, and upward movement in the stock market.

You're never going to have any use for the money you've invested in the market during a time when the market has tanked, so don't worry about that! And you're *not* going to die right in the middle of a crash or have to retire or have to pay for emergency medical care. You can afford to wait forever for the market to recover if things turn sour!

So, while those grouchy curmudgeons like Alan Abelson keep warning you, you just keep ignoring what they say while you grow richer and richer. Ha! Experience counts for very little in the stock market, my friend. Just buy, buy, buy.

27

$ $ $

Convince Yourself That You Can Beat the Market without Knowing Anything about It

What, after all, does someone like *you* even have to know about the market? The nerds and geeks may have graduate degrees. Some money managers may have decades of experience. Some pundits like Warren Buffett may have an abundance of both. But *you* have your innate gambler's luck and feel—the only cards you'll ever need. You can tell just by the way you get out of bed in the morning in which direction the market is headed. You can tell by the way the numbers are running across your computer screen whether it's an up day or a down day. You don't need a system or education or information gleaned from late hours of study—you have that feeling in your fingertips. Call it instinct, call it luck, or call it by its rightful name: genius. You can forecast the market just by the feeling in your bones.

And individual stocks? You don't need to learn how to read a 10-K or an S-1 or whatever the heck those things with the tiny little type are called. You don't have to know anything at all about accounting. Economics? Marketing? Research on business cycles or specific industries? Nonsense! Just by hearing a company's *name* you can tell if it's a winner or a loser—the same way you pick horses at the racetrack. Don't be a slave to some musty old library or some ponderous old computer. Just plunk down your money right this minute based on pure intuition.

This is definitely the way to play the market, and your way is the best way. While the other schnooks are plodding around with their tables and charts, you'll be making millions, 'cause you've got that lucky streak going—not to mention the unshakable conviction that you're always right. And that's more than enough.

28

Carve It in Stone: "Average" Returns in the Stock Market Aren't Good Enough for You!

Now, it may be true that very few of the world's money managers ever manage to "beat the market"—that is, earn better returns than the market does as a whole. There are, in fact, many scholarly studies around that prove this is true. In fact, I will go a little further and say that it may be true that even great financial geniuses can't "beat the market" for long periods. But *you* can and will, just by virtue of what you've got in the marrow of your bones!

Why should you be satisfied with "average" returns that mimic the stock market's overall trends? You're a lot better than average in every other aspect of your life (at least you think you are). So why settle for average by buying an index fund where the managers basically purchase all the big stocks in the market and then you just sit back and watch?

That might be fine for a passive, lazybones couch potato. But that ain't you. Not by a long shot. You're the kind of person who thrives on a challenge. Yes, it may be true that index funds and large (very large) mutual funds like Fidelity Magellan beat the results the ordinary small investor gets about 80 percent of the time. But so what? That has nothing to do with you.

So, don't do the easy, path-of-least-resistance thing. Get yourself psyched up to try all kinds of tricks and strategies to actually "beat the market." You're a world-beating, market-beating genius with more tricks than a dog has fleas.

And here are a few more of them. . . .

29

$ $ $

Don't Waste Your Time with a Broker Who Works for a Well-Known Firm—Go with That Nimble Little Fellow Who Sent You Spam on the Internet

The big boys, the Merrill Lynches, the Smith Barneys, the Prudentials—they're all just fossils. You need someone small and hip who can wheel and deal in and among the big old whales. You need a wily, agile guy who needs to make his bones by making you rich. That, at least to me, means someone who sent you an e-mail or a fax or maybe called you up. This is someone who isn't rich yet, but he's trying to *make* himself rich, and the only way he can do that is to make *you* rich, and then you'll tell your pals, and they'll tell *their* pals, and soon you'll all be rich.

There are some naysayers who will probably tell you that you can't trust those who make cold calls and who send you spam on the Internet. After all, who can verify their names and their reputations? But that is precisely the point, my dear friend. They are the underdogs who can spot the big opportunities before the major brokerage houses have gotten off their keesters (after their two-hour martini lunches).

So put your trust in that little guy, make him really work for you, and watch that money grow, grow, grow. Oh, by the way, haven't you ever heard of the SEC? I mentioned them a few pages back. They're on the job like white on rice, making sure that every single word sent by fax or over the Internet is totally correct and by the book. Once again, if you can't trust the government to look after you, who *can* you trust?

30

$ $ $

Act Fast! Those Stock Tips You Heard about in the Locker Room Have Real Value

I think all of us know someone who's gotten rich on a stock tip, don't we? I mean, how can we little guys (and gals) ever get to the big time if we don't act on tips and get a leg up on the competition? We don't have huge research departments. We don't have connections at the country club. No . . . but we do have friends who *hear things*. And every so often, if we're really lucky, we can *overhear* some of those things and get ourselves really well positioned to make megabucks.

Don't bother to ask how your source knows what he knows. Don't look a gift horse in the mouth by inquiring about whether any of his other "hot tips" made any money. And please don't rack your brain trying to remember if anyone ever *did* make any money as a result of a stock tip (without also going to jail, that is). No, just plunge in, and then you can laugh at all of those saps who made investments based on research and hard work while you're swimming laps in your heated Olympic-size pool.

31

$ $ $

Don't Be Satisfied to Just Buy and Hold—Rapid Trading Is the Key to wealth

If you've ever seen a movie about Wall Street (*Wall Street* is a good one!), you know very well that at the heart of this city within a city lurk men and women slaving at computer consoles, holding one phone up to each ear, shrieking "Buy!" or "Sell!" This frantic pace exemplifies how money is made in this world. It has little indeed to do with cautiously buying and holding.

Have you ever seen a movie about wealthy people on Wall Street who just sit quietly reading a novel while the investments they made ten years ago slowly grow in value? No, I don't think you have, and I don't think you ever will. Clearly, as you can see in movies and TV programs about the stock market, real money is made by trading frequently.

Think about it: How many people do you know who have quit their day jobs and then gotten rich just trading online a few hours each day at home with no guidance except the innate genius they were born with? Hundreds, I'm sure!

Buy and hold may have been fine for your grandfather's investments, but this isn't your grandfather's market. This is the new, fast-paced world of tomorrow, and you can either be in it or out of it, either make money by furious trading, or just be content being average by buying the indexes and large mutual funds and watching your life drift by down that ol' lazy river.

Some nitwits are probably going to say that there's a big difference between the way that major banks and brokerages trade, and the way that you would do it as an individual. They'll probably say that the big banks and brokerages have hedges, immense capital backing them up, and far more information than you'll ever be able to access.

Nonsense. The computer and the Internet are the great equalizers. You can do everything the big boys can do . . . and do it better and more nimbly (possibly with help from your spam-sending broker at a no-name firm!).

Don't be scared off by those horror stories about people who traded actively and lost everything. That will not happen to you. You have luck and (in fact) genius on your side, and they don't. Plus, they are not you, and that makes all the difference in the world.

32

$ $ $

Invest in Penny Stocks

Look at it this way. Suppose you buy stock in a totally unknown company, XYZ Technologies, and it's selling over the Internet for $.50 a share. Then, suppose it goes up by $.25. That means it's gone up by 50 percent—and that's real moolah!

On the other hand, if you buy GE, a company everyone is already bored with, at, say, $25, and it goes up by $.25, you've only made one percent. How are you going to make any real money that way?

Simple answer: You can't and you won't. But there's plenty of leverage in penny stocks. If they move just a tiny bit, you make a fortune. And don't worry that the same principle also works in reverse. That is, if you buy GE at $25 and it goes down by $.50, you've lost 2 percent, but if you buy XYZ at $.50 and it goes down by $.50, you've lost 100 percent.

This will never happen to you, though, because you're only buying really top-quality penny stocks, the GEs and GMs of the penny stocks—only they haven't been discovered yet.

Plus, you're only buying after you've gotten really hot tips, and when you know for sure that you're going to watch that stock zoom into the stratosphere.

So, go ahead. Live a little, pal. Swing with the penny stocks and ignore the possible pitfalls while you're riding in your pink Cadillac.

33

$ $ $

To Make Real Money, Go on Margin!

You may have never heard of "margin" except for the margins on the pages when you were taking typing class. But "margin" is an incredibly kind invention created by brokers to help make you rich.

Basically, when you "go on margin," you're borrowing money from your broker to buy extra stock you wouldn't be able to buy if you just had to pay cash for all of the stock you bought. For example, suppose you want to buy 1,000 shares of XYZ at 28, but you only have $20,000. The broker will usually lend you the other $8,000. Now, to be sure, you have to pay interest on that loan, and the interest is usually at a pretty hefty rate. But never mind that. The real truth is that you're borrowing in order to buy a stock that you and your broker just *know* will go up in value. You know it for sure. And it's bound to go up in value a lot more than the paltry interest you're paying for it, even though the interest might not seem at first blush to be so tiny on that margin account.

To clarify, if your money-market account at your brokerage house is paying eight-tenths of one percent, which is what the broker pays you when you lend him money in late 2003, that same broker will usually charge you about 7 percent to go on margin, or about nine times as much. To some whiners, that might seem like a lot. But for a smart investor like you, the story is far more apparent.

You're borrowing at 7 percent to buy a stock that you just know will double in value imminently. If that stock goes up by 100 percent, you will have only paid 7 percent to make 100 percent, leaving you with a nifty 93 percent profit—and if the stock goes up by 100 percent in a few weeks, as your picks usually will (!), you don't even have to pay all of the 7 percent margin interest. You just pay for however many days you used a 7 percent annual rate.

That means you can and do fatten your profits immensely by going on margin. It's a gift from the brokerage community. In fact, it's almost like charity.

It can get even better, though. If you're buying high-tech or biotech stocks that really swing, they can move up 200 to 300 percent in a few months—so think of the money you could make! If you just put down the minimum in cash and have all of the rest as margin (or borrowed funds), you can put rocket fuel into your portfolio. Under regulations in force as I write this, you can borrow roughly up to 50 percent of your purchase on margin.

This means you can buy twice as much as you would otherwise have bought if you'd just done the ordinary thing—that is, pay cash. *How great is that?!*

Now, as always, there will be some grouches and naysayers—I tell you, they're everywhere—who might warn you that the stock you buy is security for your margin borrowings, and if the stock falls by more than about 10 percent, you'll get an ugly thing called a "margin call." This is a phone call early in the morning that demands that you put up more money to make up for the fall in the value of your stock. That call might tell you that if you don't put up the cash right away, your position will be sold out and you'll still be liable for any difference between what you owe on the stock and what the sale brought in.

Now, some may say that they recall that in the Crash of 2000 to 2002, people who went heavily on margin ended up getting margin calls for their crashing tech stocks, couldn't come up with the cash, had the stock sold out from under them, still didn't have the funds to make up the difference, and had to sell their houses to raise the money for the margin they still owed on stocks that had become worthless or almost worthless.

But that won't ever happen to *you*, pal! You don't buy stocks that go down. You buy stocks that go up, up, and away! You'll never need to worry about a margin call because you're Mr. Lucky, and your stocks will never get closer to earth—only closer to the sun!

So, go on margin, have a great time with it, and drop me a note from your villa on the Riviera letting me know how you're doing!

34

Believe in "Black Box" Trading Methods Pitched to You by Some Wizard in a Fancy Suit

You know, there's a famous saying that goes something like this: If you're so smart, why ain't you rich? The obvious meaning of this is that smart people are rich—and know how to make *you* rich. This means that investing is, in some small way, an art, but it's largely a science. Precise scientific methods like the ones that landed a man on the moon are what we need to make the real bucks. Astrophysicists, research scientists, mathematicians who delve into quantum physics—these are the guys and gals who can make us wealthy.

So if these geniuses have some proprietary, mathematics-crammed "black box" that harnesses the power of math and the other sciences to tame the market's wild beast and make us rich in the process, why should we shy away from such a marvel? Simple answer? We shouldn't! We should grab for the gusto with both hands.

Don't worry yourself thinking about some company in Connecticut called Long-Term Capital Management and how their "black-box" methods led to a loss of billions of dollars. Don't worry about other investors who've lost their shirts to "black-box" methods that turned out to be highly fallible to say the least. *Your* black box is going to work because it's yours . . . and it's black . . . and it's a box!

35

$ $ $

Put All Your Eggs in One Basket— 'Cause Only Sissies Diversify

Now, get this straight. You, with the help of that broker you met on the Internet, your margin calls, and your innate luck, are not about to pick stocks that go down. Yours are going *up*. Knowing that, what's the point of diluting your attention and your gains by diversifying and buying lots of different stocks? Why give yourself a lot of confusing things to think about and a lot of extra lines on your financial statements?

No, put all of your eggs in that basket that's marked "For Winners Only"! Maybe do the thing that's easiest and involves the path of least resistance:

Put all of your money into the stock of the company that employs you. Often, that company will sell you its stock at a bargain rate, considerably below the market price. And you know it's a good company—otherwise you wouldn't be there, you dog, you! So, yes, definitely put all of your eggs in that one basket and watch them hatch and turn out golden geese!

Diversification? We don't need no stinkin' diversification!

36

$$ \$ \$ \$ $$

Ignore Investment Fees and Expenses—They're Just Nickels and Dimes

So what if your mutual fund charges you 6 percent or 4 percent or 3 percent to get into it. Who the heck cares? Those are just a few pennies out of every dollar. So what if you could've bought an almost identical mutual fund for "no load" (no fees) or no commission on the sale at all? These are just tiny sums. They'll never add up to a thing.

And so what if your broker is charging you 2 percent on the price of the stocks with a $200 minimum charge? That's just 2 percent out of every dollar.

When your stock has doubled, you won't remember the cost of that commission one little bit.

None of those costs will ever add up to a thing compared with the billions you'll make on your investments. So just pay whatever the brokers or the mutual funds charge. Hey, they have to eat, too, right? And you want them to be happy and fat and sleek; otherwise, how will they ever be in a good enough mood to make any real money for you? (And don't worry about such esoterica and trivia as "market timing" or "late trading" by the managers of your mutual funds. They may look unethical and crooked, but that's just because you are innocent and naive. There's really nothing at all wrong with any of those things, so don't worry your pretty little head about it.)

Worrywarts and nerds and prissy-pants investors worry about those few cents on the dollar that go toward fees and charges. But swingin' cats like you who make billions and live in mansions and cruise on yachts didn't get there by worrying about a few cents here and there.

Hey, if you're going to worry about every nickel and dime, maybe you shouldn't be investing your money at all!

37

$ $ $

Buy and Read Newsletters about Investing, and Do Exactly What They Say

Publishing a newsletter about the stock market is no small feat. It takes a hefty amount of knowledge, education, experience, and street savvy. They don't let just *anyone* do these things. You have to be someone who's been around the market a long time and has made tons of money consistently for oneself and for one's readers— only then will the FTC or the SEC (or whoever regulates newsletters) allow the guy or gal to write and sell the publication.

You can trust anyone who passes this rigorous test and believe every word he writes.

Wait just a freaking minute! What's that, you say? You heard that there *are basically no* FTC or SEC regulations for people writing and publishing financial newsletters? That anyone can do it anytime he or she feels like it? Well, maybe, but so what? They do have to fill out some forms, don't they? Isn't that enough?

The investment business is populated by men and women of only the highest moral character. Those who take on the awesome responsibility of advising others would not do so lightly. They would have to feel in their heart and soul that they could do the job properly, that they had the right credentials, and that they had a long history of making money in all kinds of markets.

And so what if the "data" shows that newsletter writers are usually wrong and, in fact, you can usually make more money by doing just the opposite of what they advise?

Well, none of this applies to you . . . *because you're only going to read the newsletter that's always right.* And how will you know which one that is? Never mind. You'll just know. So go ahead and read to your heart's content, and plunk down your very last dime investing in what the writers recommend. You'll be up there with the Rockefellers in no time flat!

38

$ $ $

Make Sure You Never Hold Your Financial Adviser or Broker Accountable—You Want Him to Be Your Friend

There are measurements that come out regularly in *Barron's, The Wall Street Journal,* and many other fine financial publications about how well the stock market has done in the past six months, the past year, or the past five years. They track broad market indexes like the S&P 500 and the Dow Jones 30 Industrials.

Please don't make your financial adviser's life difficult by comparing his picks and suggestions with this broad gauge. You only need to know that he's your pal, that he takes your calls promptly, and basically, that's it. If he's a friend to you, talks to you, reassures you, and maybe occasionally takes you to lunch and picks up the tab, you know he's your kind of guy. Don't make him feel bad if other measurements are going up faster than your investments. He's a nice family man with a good personality. That's enough.

39

If Your Investment Program Isn't Producing Good Results, Keep Doing the Same Thing Anyway

You might have heard the old saying, "If nothing changes, then nothing changes." That means that if you keep doing what you've *been* doing, then you'll get the same results you've always gotten.

Some might tell you that this applies in spades to your investments. If you keep doing the same thing, you might keep getting the same results. But, that's not true for you. If by some weird fluke your investments (recommended by your no-name broker, your friends on the Internet, newsletter writers, infomercial spokespersons, and the tips you overheard at the gym) don't do well for a few years, just keep doing the same thing—that is, investing based on suggestions from those same sources—and sure enough, those investments will turn the corner and start rocketing up.

With the exception of the ones that have gone bankrupt and stopped trading, of course. Those probably won't recover, but for you, they might come back and start dancing on their graves and make you some money.

So just go with the flow, and don't worry, be happy. Wait a few more years to check on how you're doing. In the meantime, let it flow, let it flow.

And this leads to the next item, as vital as any other for ruining your financial life . . .

40

$$\$\ \$\ \$$

If Taking Charge of Your Financial Life Seems Overwhelming Now, Just Put It Off for a Few More Years

There's this old myth that says you should get movin' right now on accomplishing your goals, because the more time you have to work on them, the more likely you are to attain them. And then there's some old saw about how a journey is more likely to get finished if you start early in the morning.

What a load of bull! Didn't the idiots who came up with those maxims realize how much fun it is to sleep late? Didn't they know that some days are just for kicking back and having a few martinis and watching the sunset?

It takes a lot of mental effort to take charge of your finances. If it seems a bit burdensome right now, just wait a while until it seems like it would be less of a bother. Only when you're really and truly up to it should you get yourself in gear to make plans for your financial future. Don't worry about the time that passed while you were getting yourself organized. I'm sure it was good for something—if only for sleeping late, you movie star, you!

41

$ $ $

Start a Business with Inadequate Capital—in a Difficult Field and in a Difficult Location— and Expect to Prosper

This essay could just as well be called "Open a Restaurant," which is surely one of the best ways on earth to lose a ton of money, your spouse, and your peace of mind. But don't let that thought worry you. No, forget what I just wrote. I was just kidding.

But, seriously, why don't you open a restaurant in an area where millions of other people have started eateries that went out of business. Go ahead. It'll be fine. Where everyone else—even people with experience—went down the tubes, you'll succeed just because of your innate charisma.

Besides, restaurants are really easy businesses to run. I mean, haven't you ever seen *Casablanca?* Humphrey Bogart is always in a dinner jacket or a suit, is never in a hurry, and never has to face problems with customers or waiters who don't show up or waitresses who have to leave early for an audition. Owners of restaurants lead carefree lives, just lounging on the chaise while the money rolls in on top of them.

So start a restaurant—or any business where the failure rate is 90 percent or more—and you'll be amazed to see how easy and fun it is and how much money you make. You won't need to worry about burning through all your cash in a few months and being overwhelmed by debt. Nope, not you—'cause you won't make the same mistakes those other suckers made.

You know better.

42

$ $ $

Don't Worry about Buying Stocks When There's a Bubble Going On—You'll Always Know when to Sell Out Just Before the Bubble Bursts

There are a lot of old-fashioned measurements that tell old fogeys when stocks are cheap and when they're expensive by historic measurements. These are ways to calculate the ratio of the stock's price with respect to its earnings and dividends. When these get really, really high—when stocks are flying—those measurements are really high, too, and some curmudgeons call those times "bub-bles" and tell you to stay away from buying stocks then.

What nonsense that is! When stocks are high-flyin', that's when it's the most fun to be in the stock market! How much fun is it to invest when stocks barely move at all, or at most, a few percent a year? It's BO-RING. But when stocks are really soaring, and when they've cut their ties to history and earth and common sense, that's when you pick up the stock page of the newspaper or go online and find out that your tech stock has doubled within the last week. That's when you really feel super-duper rich and smart.

So, why listen to the old creeps who tell you to beware when the stock market is at those levels? Why even pay a moment's attention? If, in fact, the bubble is bound to burst, you'll know about it and get out in plenty of time.

Uh, *how* will you know? Well, hasn't Warren Buffett said that in a bubble, everyone says they'll leave the party at midnight, only there are no clocks in the room? Yes, but so what? You don't invest based on clocks and old fuddy-duddy rules. You invest by the intuitive feelings in your fingertips, and those feelings will also tell you when—exactly when—to sell, take your profits, and go hang out at Cap d'Antibes.

So, go ahead. Buy at the peak. You'll never regret it, not for a moment. Bubbles are fun for you because you, and only you, know when to get in and when to get out.

Now, let's leave the stock market and investing behind. After all, the market isn't the only game in town. Let's try some other ways for you to get rich quick (and ruin your financial life). . . .

43

$ $ $

If Getting Your Finances Together Seems Too Difficult at Any Given Time, Turn Everything Over to a Financial/Business Manager Who Will Have Total Control Over Your Money

Hey, why worry about nickels and dimes and boring things like IRAs and Keoghs and how much money to save? Why fill out dusty old forms for the IRS or the state income-tax board? Why not have some gal with a green eyeshade and sleeve garters take care of all that for you?

My advice is to find some trustworthy person who claims to be well versed in money management, go to her office with your checkbook and a power of attorney, and turn everything over to her. In this world, you can only trust a few select people with your money, but you'll unerringly find the right one. A suggestion? Go for the one who charges the most. Don't be happy with anyone who charges you less than 5 percent. Maybe even pay a few percentage points more for quality service.

Then, just send all your bills to her and have her pay them, let her withdraw money from your accounts for investments, and generally allow her to do everything but the heavy lifting. And don't feel lazy for doing it. Many busy, important people like you have better things to do than worry about stuffy old money matters.

You may have heard those horror stories about financial managers who looted their clients mainly because these folks were too lazy to pay any attention to their financial statements. You may have also heard stories about horribly mangled billing statements from credit-card companies and department stores that some business manager's semiliterate assistant paid anyway and the money could never be recovered. You may have heard of financial managers who made terrible mistakes in their investment decisions for one client and then looted their other clients to cover it up.

Pay no attention to any of this at all. It will never happen to you. If you can't trust someone with a nice office and a smooth patter to handle your money, who can you trust?

Besides, untended pots of money are not really *that* big a temptation to wicked minds, are they? Certainly not. So go right ahead and live it up while your financial manager takes over the reins. There will never be a day of reckoning for trusting your future to someone whose interests might totally differ from yours and who might have the ethics of a snake.

And if you believe that one . . .

44

Believe That You Can Get Rich Quick—That You Can Get Something for Nothing

There *are* such things as free lunches!

This one is so obvious that I don't think I need to say much about it. It's simply a statement of truth that a smart guy or gal like you was born knowing.

Basically, real riches appear overnight just by luck or chance or a bolt of inspiration (see the next essay). You don't need to trade experience or labor or investments for wealth. If you're on the right track, you'll reap the financial rewards overnight . . . money will rain down on your house in torrents.

Let me explain this a little further . . .

45

Know Without a Doubt That You Don't Have to Work Hard— You Only Need to Find an Angle

Get hip to life. Hard work is for suckers. Manual labor is for losers and fools. How often have you seen impecunious (look it up) old people who have worked and slaved all of their lives and are still broke? Or at least not rich. And how many of your pals work year in and year out and just get tiny little pay raises (or none at all) and never get ahead?

The truth of this realization is painful but then liberating: *Hard work gets you nowhere slowly.* It's for those without imagination.

But *you* are different. You have that creative spark. You have that special magic that's going to make you wake up one morning at 4 A.M., shout out, "Eureka!" and have the brainstorm that will bring you staggering wealth.

What will the inspiration be? Well, if I knew, I'd be as rich as you're going to be, wouldn't I? And I'm not, am I? So what will it be? The next Velcro? A new computer program that lets people actually make love through the Internet? A perfume for dogs that allows them to smell as good as they look? A dating service for sex addicts? A formula that decodes the Bible and tells you when to buy stocks and when to sell?

You may not know what will come to you just yet, but the thing to remember is that if you hang out on the sofa most of the time, watch a lot of TV reruns, eat as much junk food as you can, and maybe smoke a few bong loads . . . then the light-bulb will surely go off. All at once, you'll vault over all of those hardworking geeks who seemed as if they'd completely outpace you. You'll rocket to success in a matter of weeks.

So don't bother to work hard. Just take a lot of naps and wait for that flash of lightning to explode in your brain. The world is waiting breathlessly for you to come down from the mountaintop with your two tablets and your inspiration that will make the Ten Commandments seem comically insignificant.

Go for it. You just need that one clever angle.

46

$ $ $

Do Not Buy a Home—a Free Spirit Like You Does Not Need to Put Down Roots

Let's face it—owning a home is a heap of trouble. You have to save up for the down payment (and I think I already told you *not* to save because it takes money away from the fun stuff you'd like to spend it on, such as vacations and clothes and cars and stereo equipment). So that's a problem.

Then you have to do something really abhorrent. You have to obligate yourself to pay off a mortgage that could last as long as 30 years. That's right. You have to promise—in blood, practically—that you'll make a large payment to the bank or mortgage company every damned month for three whole decades.

How much fun is that? Who in their right mind wants to be that tied down? I don't. Do you?

And then what about the maintenance and the upkeep? If you live in a rental, all you have to do is call the super when there's a backed-up toilet. But if you own your own home, hey, pal, you have to get out the plunger yourself. If you have rats, you can't just call the landlord and yell at him. You have to get out the rat poison and the cats and go after those wicked little rodents.

And what if the roof leaks? What do you do then? Plus, there's fire insurance, flood insurance, earthquake insurance if you live in California, liability insurance—it goes on and on. Then there's painting—and I haven't even gotten to the landscaping yet, which is a major, *major* hassle all unto itself. Until you own a home, you just have no freaking clue how much work it is. In fact, it's too much work. That's the bottom line.

And have I even mentioned termites? Do you know what a disaster they can be? But they're just one small part of the burden of home ownership.

Why do it? Oh, sure, a home may go up in value and allow your small down payment to build into a huge equity pool. So what? Is that worth having to find a plumber at 7 in the morning on a Sunday?

Yes, you do get immense tax subsidies for owning a home and financing it with a mortgage. So? I already told you not to pay taxes!

It's true that for most people, their homes become their biggest asset and help cushion ups and downs in the stock market or in their jobs. But that means zero to you. You're a troubadour. A hippie. A free bird. You don't need to concern yourself with the trivialities of mundane money grubbing. You want your landlord to worry about repairs and paint and termites. *You* worry about things like whether Britney Spears will ever get back with Justin Timberlake. You worry about whether your local supermarket will start carrying that beer you like. You worry about that scratch on your car.

Let others make their stupid profits and capital gains from their homes. If they want to convert themselves into adding machines, that's their problem—not yours. Just stay ready to hit the road any old time the feeling strikes you. No home ownership for poets and prophets like you.

Nope. No way.

47

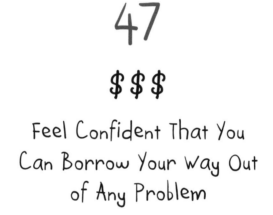

Feel Confident That You Can Borrow Your Way Out of Any Problem

You know how I've been telling you over and over that you don't need to save money? Well, some of you (who haven't been listening very well) may have had a sneaking little thought enter your minds: *What if I suddenly need money? How will I handle it if I don't have any money saved up?*

Good question, and it has a good answer: You *borrow* the money when you need it by getting a cash advance on your credit cards. The interest rate is only about 20 percent. Sometimes it's lower, sometimes higher, but the banks that issue credit cards are only too happy to lend you money any old time you please. Cash advances are a breeze to get and very easy to spend.

Or, go to a finance company and get a signature loan. (Remember, you don't have a home to borrow on, right?) Those unsecured loans are really great things, too. They also charge a bit of interest, but what the heck. If you need the money, who cares about the interest?

And here's a sneaky little tip: There are also special friends out there who will want to lend you money. True, many people make it a practice *not* to lend money. But not your best pals. They can and will lend you money and tide you over any rough spots. That's what they're there for. Don't even think about being too embarrassed to ask for a loan—or worrying about your buddies' discomfort over being asked. Just ask for it—in fact, even demand it! What are friends for? They've probably been boring and practical enough to save, so what's the point of saving if not to do nice things for other people? So, go for it. Your pals will be happy to oblige—it might even strengthen your friendship.

And here's another word of advice: When you get that borrowed money, *don't repay it.* Think about it for a moment. How are you any better off if you borrow a thousand bucks and then a few weeks later *repay* a thousand bucks? You're in exactly the same position you were before. But if you borrow the thousand and then don't repay it, or only repay a little of it, you've made a profit! It's like it was a gift. So, borrow, allow your pals to feel good about helping you out, and then go on your merry way.

Borrowing your way out of a jam is really the only smart maneuver. Bear this in mind!

48

$ $ $

Rest Assured That Shopping Is a Perfectly Valid Form of Emotional and Physical Exercise— Whether You Need What You're Buying or Not

It feels good to shop. You go into a store, you get people to wait on you, you try things on, you see something really cute, and you buy it. And you feel like a new person. Not only that, but you get out of the house and see people. You get to call the shots because *you're* the one throwing money around while simpering lackeys cater to your every whim.

Plus, you get exercise walking from store to store. That's good for those buttocks, calves, and thighs, dontcha know.

And while we're at it, please keep in mind a few additional points on why shopping is so beneficial for you:

- Goods bought at retail have some value and cost something, but goods bought on sale at steep discounts are free!

- Clothes bearing fancy labels are far better than those with generic brand names—even if they look exactly the same and have the identical fabric content. And designer clothes bought in one of those brand-names-for-less stores shouldn't even be considered. Only clothes you buy at full price are worth holding on to for a long time.

- Don't stop to think about whether you really need all the items you're splurging on, on any particular day. If you like something and it fits, it means you need it and should buy it.

Sold!

49

Carefully Pore Over All Those Catalogs You Get in the Mail, and Order from Them Late at Night or When You're Feeling Lonely

You can really cheer your bad self up by ordering something when you're alone at home at night. Maybe your girlfriend or boyfriend just gave you a hard time (perhaps by asking for that money back that you borrowed last month). Maybe you're feeling a little down in the dumps as you lie in bed and pet your kitty. But don't worry. Just call up the catalog companies and buy some things you don't really need. The customer-service agents at those companies will be overjoyed to help you out, and they'll treat you with the respect you deserve after a hard day.

Not only that, but if it's really late at night, you'll have someone with a friendly voice to chat with!

Who cares if you don't even bother to open the boxes once they're delivered? As long as you know that those items are waiting patiently in your garage or closet for you, that's all that matters. You can get to them someday when you're good and ready, and it will be like Christmas in the middle of May.

And the real pleasure of catalog ordering isn't actually getting the merchandise. It's ordering it— and once you've done that, you can sleep like a baby. (Until you get the bill, that is.)

50

$ $ $

Don't Sweat the Small Stuff— After All, $10 or $20 a Day Doesn't Really Add Up to Much!

That's right. Keep buying three or four coffee drinks at Starbucks every day during the week. So what if it's $15 or $20 a day, every single day? What does that even amount to? Five to seven thousand dollars a year? Who cares?

Those few thousands here and there don't mean a damned thing, so don't even think about them at all. You're not some little mole burrowed in a cave pinching pennies. You're a free spirit, as I keep saying. If a couple of caffe mochas served up by a college-age cutie make the difference for you today . . . and tomorrow . . . and the next day . . . then go for it!

51

$ $ $

Find a Man or Woman with Really Expensive Tastes and Reckless Financial Habits— and Marry Him or Her!

One must avoid being lonely at all costs, so you need to have someone in your life at all times. And what better person to live with than someone who recklessly spends your money? These are the people who will buy fun things for themselves or for you (with your dough), who insist on taking lavish vacations, and who toss around $100 bills (yours) as if they were Pringles potato chips.

But don't just hang around with these kinds of people—marry one of them! Your mate (let's say it's a woman for the sake of example) will quickly find many new, fun ways to squander money—and again, what else is more fun? Maybe she'll find ways to gamble your money away (we haven't even gotten to that one yet!), charge extravagantly on your credit cards, "lose" money that you give her to buy groceries, and just somehow find a way to make your little domestic ship of financial well-being capsize.

Don't even think about marrying some cautious little squirrel who saves money and never spends any of it. Those people are dull, unsexy, dictatorial wet blankets. Instead of that, only associate with the fun people who like to spend, and see where that takes you. *Hint:* I guarantee it will keep you up at night.

52

$ $ $

Get Separated
and Divorced Frequently

It doesn't really cost that much to get divorced.
You just have to divide every single freakin' thing
you own in half and give it away. But what do
you care? You're not a scale. You're not a balance
sheet. You're a soul who has to be happy no matter
what the cost—and be damned with trying to work
things out! It's better to lose half of what you own
and have to pay alimony and child support—or
receive those things and lose your house—than to
tolerate even a second's worth of discomfort.

In fact, you should be *looking* for reasons to get
divorced. There will always be plenty of them if you

look hard enough. It stirs the pot to keep things moving in your life. It keeps you on your toes. You won't get complacent.

So what if a couple of divorce settlements can cripple even the most affluent man or woman? Your independence and self-respect are worth a heck of a lot more than mere money. And what about compromise and turning the other cheek? Well, maybe that's all right for losers and weaklings, but not for you. You demand your freedom and your dignity, and if you have to pay a lot for it, it's well worth that sordid money. You'll always make a lot more now that you're not tied down anyway.

And by the way, you're really going to be thrilled to see how reasonable divorce lawyers are. They hardly charge a dime. For the most part, they just want to help you out of a difficult patch in your life and don't care about money at all.

(And all of this doesn't even take into account how much fun it is to be alone—especially when you're wrinkled, saggy and middle-aged!)

53

Don't Keep Records

No record keeping for you! That's for librarians and bookkeepers and hermits. And anyway, since you're never going to have a financial plan and are never going to need money for retirement, why would you need to keep records?

Look at it this way. Suppose it's a nice, relaxing evening. You could spend it on the deck of your apartment drinking daiquiris, you could use the time to watch *Jimmy Kimmel Live* on TV, you could make some calls to your friends to tell them about the creepy date you had last night . . . or, you could spend your time filing statements from your bank or broker while standing next to some rusty old file cabinet.

Which sounds like more fun? And when that time comes when the IRS asks for your records for the last five years, just tell them that you're not a clerk and you don't have no wicked records, man! They'll understand.

Plus, if your broker makes a mistake and you don't have the records to prove she's wrong, so what? The IRS will just take your word for it. Just have another cocktail and another buffalo chicken wing and soon you won't even remember that it's almost tax time—oh, but that's right, you don't pay taxes.

Ah, life is good!

54

$ $ $

Gamble with Your Money

This may seem a bit obvious, but let me explain. It seems that a lot of otherwise decent folks are just scared to gamble with their money. This is silly. It's a great deal of fun to visit a casino or a racetrack and plunk down your dough . . . and then let Lady Luck have her way with you.

Casinos and racetracks are fascinating places. There are lots of good-looking men and women, as well as food stands and restaurants and bars to eat and drink in—basically, a good time just waiting to happen. And there's also the chance—in your case, a certainty—of making a heap o' cash. The roulette wheel, if you play it right, pays off something like

36 to one. Those are much better odds than working for 40 years!

And the racetrack? Have you ever heard of a prefecta? A trifecta? Do you have any clue how much they can pay off? It can be stupendous. Thousands to one. You can go in with a $5 ticket and walk out with enough money to buy a house . . . if you were foolish enough to buy a house.

Why forego that pleasure? Why not gamble your money on the possibility that your life could suddenly change on a dime (or a two-dollar ticket!) or a card in a blackjack hand or even seven numbers in a lottery? Why not give yourself a shot at doing something truly magnificent with only a few dollars down?

And let's not forget sports betting. It's thrilling! You know what I mean—that adrenaline rush you get when you realize that if your team doesn't make a touchdown you'll lose $10,000! But if you do win . . . wow, you could be set for a long time! So why not make bets on as many games as you can? What could possibly be more rewarding than spending a Sunday watching three TVs with a different football game on each, knowing that you have money riding on every one of them? I mean, when you think about it, it's really no fun at all to just watch a game without betting on it—that's for losers! And when you win big and the bookie sends over your money, hey, champ, that's when things really start to sizzle!

So, go for it, pal, live it up, and have fun, fun, fun—and also know in your heart that you're really helping people out, too. You're probably aware that gambling is one of the few rapidly growing businesses in this country—heck, Native American tribes depend on it for their livelihood! And there wouldn't be any gleaming palaces in Las Vegas without gambling. Atlantic City, in fact, would still be a pitiful backwater without it.

So have yourself a great time and know that you're helping Native American children get scholarships; that you're contributing to the construction of gorgeous buildings in the desert; that you're providing employment for card dealers, showgirls, and hookers . . . and that you're lighting the candle that shoots you to the moon, baby, to the moon!

55

$ $ $

Don't Bother to Provide for Your Spouse or Your Children

Why should you do anything for posterity? What the heck has posterity ever done for you? Aren't your kids always asking for things? Aren't they a pain in the neck? Why should you feel that you owe them a thing? Wouldn't they be better off anyway if they had to work for everything they got, like Abe Lincoln or Andrew Carnegie?

Don't bother sacrificing one single thing for your kids or your spouse so that they'll be better off or well provided for when you die. What will it mean to you? You'll be dead anyway. Why should you have to sacrifice a trip or a new boat to buy insurance for your family? It's all about you, you, you, anyway, and once you're gone, the world ends, too. What possible concern could it be of yours that your spouse or kids might have to scrimp and save when you're gone? They're only your flesh and blood.

What about setting up accounts for your kids so they can pay for college or make a down payment on a home? No way. There are scholarships. There are student loans and jobs. Or they can go without college. It might do them good to go out and work right after high school. Why coddle them with money when you could have so much more fun coddling yourself?

So basically, just devote your life to thinking about your own wants and needs, and let the chips fall where they may.

But you knew all this already, didn't you? You're a real winner— through and through!

$ $ $

AFTERWORD

$ $ $

Well, all righty then. If you've read this far, it's just possible that you have some idea what you're doing wrong. It just may be the case that you've noticed you're doing a lot of the aforementioned ruinous things that spell T-R-O-U-B-L-E in your financial life. It could be that you're not saving regularly. Perhaps you're supporting three households due to your frequent divorces. Maybe you plunk down money on stocks based on overheard tips and rumors. Most likely, you simply have no plan whatsoever and prefer not to think about your finances at all.

Well, let me assure you that if you just keep on doing what you're doing, things will only get worse. I've said it before in this book and I'll say it again: "If nothing changes, nothing changes." If you keep doing even a few of the 55 things I've mentioned, you're going to wind up in drastic circumstances down the road—or you'll remain there if that's your situation now.

But if you just start doing a few of the following, you might be amazed at the difference it makes in your life:

- Save as much as you can on a regular basis.

- Invest conservatively—for example, in very broad stock-market indexes, variable annuities, and short-term broad-based mutual funds, Treasury or high-grade corporate bonds.

- Buy your own home, buy your own home, buy your own home, buy your own home, buy your own home.

- Avoid doing business with people unless they have a good reputation for probity and integrity, and if you can't find out anything about them, don't let them anywhere near your money!

- Remember that spending is not a substitute for saving.

- Remind yourself continually that life goes by with stunning, breathtaking speed, and you will want to prepare for the day when you no longer have the strength to work—or at least to work as hard as you did when you were young—and such preparation primarily takes the form of saving.

- Leave fancy gimmicks to stupid people.

- Know that there are no free lunches anywhere once your parents die, that you are the primary person responsible for you, and that caring for your family is a moral duty—and this includes being careful with your money.

Or, to boil it all down to an even denser soup, here are two final pieces of advice: The first one is from my father and he said it to me with love—and just the fact that he thought I would understand it was a high tribute. "Benjy," he said, "live prudently."

I don't do it often enough, but I do it occasionally.

The other remark, even simpler, is from Bernard Baruch, that Wise Man of money who advised Presidents on financial matters for 40 years. After World War I, he was asked what advice he had for Americans in the new postwar world. He replied simply, "Work and save."

$ $ $

ABOUT THE AUTHOR

Ben Stein is a graduate of Columbia University and Yale Law School. He has worked as a speechwriter for Presidents Nixon and Ford, a columnist and editorial writer for *The Wall Street Journal,* a law instructor at Pepperdine University, and a teacher of media studies at American University in Washington, D.C., and the University of California at Santa Cruz. He has written for *The American Spectator* for 30 years, and speaks throughout the country on a regular basis. He is probably best known for his acting roles in *Ferris Bueller's Day Off* and *The Wonder Years* and for his long-running Emmy Award–winning game show, *Win Ben Stein's Money.* Ben is the author of numerous books, is a frequent television commentator, and lives in Los Angeles with his wife, Alexandra; and his son, Thomas.

Website: **www.benstein.com**

NOTES

◈ ◈ ◈ NOTES ◈ ◈ ◈

 NOTES

NOTES

NOTES

◈ ◈ ◈ NOTES ◈ ◈ ◈

◈ ◈ ◈ NOTES ◈ ◈ ◈

NOTES

Hay House Titles of Related Interest

※ ※ ※

All of the above are available at your local bookstore,
or may be ordered by visiting Hay House (see next page)

We hope you enjoyed this Hay House book.
If you'd like to receive a free catalog featuring additional
Hay House books and products, or if you'd like information
about the Hay Foundation, please contact:

Hay House, Inc.
P.O. Box 5100
Carlsbad, CA 92018-5100

(760) 431-7695 or **(800) 654-5126**
(760) 431-6948 (fax) or **(800) 650-5115 (fax)**
www.hayhouse.com

Published and distributed in Australia by: Hay House Australia Pty. Ltd. • 18/36 Ralph St. • Alexandria NSW 2015 • *Phone:* 612-9669-4299 • *Fax:* 612-9669-4144 • www.hayhouse.com.au

Published and distributed in the United Kingdom by:
Hay House UK, Ltd. • Unit 62, Canalot Studios •
222 Kensal Rd., London W10 5BN • *Phone:* 44-20-8962-1230 •
Fax: 44-20-8962-1239 • www.hayhouse.co.uk

Published and distributed in the Republic of South Africa by: Hay House SA (Pty), Ltd., P.O. Box 990, Witkoppen 2068 • *Phone/Fax:* 27-11-706-6612 • orders@psdprom.co.za

Distributed in Canada by: Raincoast •
9050 Shaughnessy St., Vancouver, B.C. V6P 6E5 •
Phone: (604) 323-7100 • *Fax:* (604) 323-2600

Tune in to **www.hayhouseradio.com**™ for the best in inspirational talk radio featuring top Hay House authors! And, sign up via the Hay House USA Website to receive the Hay House online newsletter and stay informed about what's going on with your favorite authors. You'll receive bimonthly announcements about: Discounts and Offers, Special Events, Product Highlights, Free Excerpts, Giveaways, and more!
www.hayhouse.com